If you are depressed you probably don't feel much like reading a book. You're not alone. Most people experiencing depression experience low energy and trouble concentrating. I have written this book with this in mind. It's short, clear and to-the point. I think you'll find it practical and easy to read.

Whether you purchase this book or not *please* know:

Depression is:

- Very common (affecting ten percent of all people each year and one in five over the life span).
- Very serious — can cause tremendous suffering and can last for months, if untreated.
- But, depression is *very* treatable.

Yet only one-third of depressed people seek treatment!

I hope this book will help – but if you do nothing else, please seek treatment now! Call your local mental health association for referrals or talk to your family doctor. *Take action now.* There are ways that you can beat depression.

— John Preston

For More Information About Depression Please Contact:

Depression Awareness (D/ART) Program
National Institute of Mental Health
5600 Fishers Lane, Room 10-85
Rockville, MD 20857
For Free Brochure, Call D/ART: 1-800-421-4211
or Visit: WWW.NIMH.NIH.GOV

National Mental Health Association
1021 Prince Street
Alexandria, VA 22314-2971
Phone: 1-800-969-NMHA   Web: WWW.NMHA.ORG

You can beat depression

You can beat depression

FOURTH EDITION

A GUIDE TO PREVENTION & RECOVERY

DR. JOHN PRESTON

***Impact Publishers*®**
ATASCADERO, CALIFORNIA

First Edition, 1989
Second Edition, 1996
Third Edition, 2001
Fourth Edition, 2004
Copyright © 1989, 1996, 2001, 2004
by John Preston
Second Printing, April, 2007

ATTENTION ORGANIZATIONS AND CORPORATIONS:
This book is available at quantity discounts on bulk purchases for educational, business, or sales promotional use. For further information, please contact Impact Publishers, P.O. Box 6016, Atascadero, California 93423-6016. Phone 805-466-5917, e-mail: info@impactpublishers.com

Library of Congress Cataloging-in-Publication Data

Preston, John, 1950-
  You can beat depression : a guide to prevention & recovery / John Preston. — 4th ed.
    p. cm.
  Includes bibliographical references and index.
  ISBN 1-886230-60-9 (alk. paper)
  1. Depression, Mental —Popular works. I. Title.
RC537.P694 2004
616.85'27—dc22   2004009045

Impact Publishers and colophon are registered trademarks of Impact Publishers, Inc.

Cover design by Sharon Wood Schnare, San Luis Obispo, California.
Printed in the United States of America on acid-free paper.
Published by *Impact* 🐾 *Publishers*®
POST OFFICE BOX 6016
ATASCADERO, CALIFORNIA 93423-6016
www.impactpublishers.com

Dedication

For David and Rachal.

Contents

Acknowledgements

I wish to acknowledge the pioneering efforts of Drs. Albert Ellis, Aaron Beck, John Rush and David Burns. Their insights and innovations have sparked new hopes for people suffering from depression.

Special appreciation to Isabel Davidoff and the members of NIMH's Depression Awareness program. This marvelous program is making a difference in the public's perception of depression as a treatable condition. My editor, Dr. Robert Alberti, has provided numerous helpful suggestions. His help is deeply appreciated.

Special thanks to two good friends and colleagues: Dr. John O'Neal and Dr. Mike Duveneck. Their encouragement, support and love have sustained me.

To Bonnie, my wife: Thanks for spending your life with me and sharing our goals to reduce human suffering.

Finally, I wish to express tremendous gratitude to my patients, who have taught me how to survive and how to grow.

— John Preston, Psy.D

Author's Note

To the best of my knowledge, recommended doses for antidepressant medications listed in this book are accurate. However, they are not meant to serve as a guide for prescription medications. Physicians, please check the manufacturer's product information sheet or the Physician's Desk Reference for any changes in dosage schedule or contraindications.

All patient's names and cases mentioned in this book have been disguised to protect their privacy and confidentiality.

Publisher's Note

This publication is designed to provide accurate and authoritative information in regard to the subject matter covered. It is sold with the understanding that the publisher is not engaged in rendering psychological, medical, or other professional services. If expert assistance or counseling is needed, the services of a competent professional should be sought.

Introduction

Introduction

Depression is painful.

It's a disabling condition that affects millions of people each year, causing tremendous emotional distress, interfering with daily living, family life, and work, increasing the risk of physical illness, and sometimes even leading to suicide. However, as I'll make clear in this book, depression is a very treatable condition. Unfortunately, most depressed people are not treated and are unaware of the help that is available.

One of the most painful aspects of depression is the sense of helplessness and powerlessness that depressed people often feel. You may be experiencing it as a sense of being trapped, unable to overcome profound feelings of despair and hopelessness. Concerned friends may try to cheer you up by saying "Things will get better . . . look on the bright side . . ." Most of the time such words of encouragement do little to pierce the veil of sadness and pessimism. True hope can only be sparked when you find out about ways to beat depression that make sense to you and that have been shown to be effective.

In this book I'll present to you, in a brief and easy to understand way, several approaches to the treatment of depression for adults and older teenagers. All these methods have solid and sound scientific evidence of effectiveness. The ideas fall into two broad categories: *professional treatment* and *self-help approaches*. Many people who are depressed need and can benefit significantly from treatment with a mental health professional. But there is a lot you can do to gain control over your depression on your own, and a self-help approach can pay extra benefits:

• You may notice positive results in a relatively short time, since the self-help approaches described here are extremely effective; there is ample research to show that they *work*.

• There is a special sense of satisfaction and power that can be experienced when you are able to do certain things, notice that it makes a difference, and know in your own mind that you are in control and have the ability to combat depressed feelings. Restoring a sense of personal power and increased self-confidence/self-esteem is an important part of overcoming depression.

• These self-help approaches can also be very helpful for people who are involved in professional treatment.

• As a bonus, once you have learned specific skills for reducing your depression, you have gained tools which will allow you to ward off the recurrence of depression.

• Self-help is *not a substitute* for professional treatment, of course. Apply the insights and ideas you gain from this book, but be sure to get professional help if you need it. Chapters 4 and 13 will help you decide.

I realize that for many people experiencing depression, even the idea of reading a book can feel like a difficult task. I want to make this process easier and have attempted to write a book that is brief easy to understand. The first chapter addresses the question, "What is depression?" The following chapters will focus on how to cope and when to seek out professional treatment.

It is my sincere hope that this book will make a difference for you — or someone in your life . . .

Part One:

Understanding Depression

1

What Is Depression?

I f you are depressed, it is likely that you have tried many things to feel better. Depression is hard to shake. So many times people try to ward off the unpleasant feelings, the fatigue, the apathy, and the hopelessness, only to feel frustrated and powerless.

In the psychiatry department of a large west coast medical center, I developed a depression management clinic in which people are taught what depression is, what causes it, how to cope with it, and how professional treatment can help. Approximately 2500 people attended our depression management classes in the first three years. I talked with many of these people after attending the classes and conducted extensive follow-up interviews. We found that the classes offer considerable help and hope for depressed people.

Some of the most common comments made by patients after attending the class:

"Now I understand what's been happening to me. I thought I was going crazy. I wish someone had explained to me earlier what depression is all about."

"For the first time in a long while I have a feeling of hope . . . I feel like I have something specific I can do now to reduce my depression."

"The self-help techniques make sense to me."

One lady who attended the class twice announced,

"I didn't think anything could help me. I was skeptical and felt hopeless. But after the last class I attended, I tried the self-help approaches and they work. I'm back here again to get a booster shot so I can keep from getting depressed again."

In preparing the class and in writing this book I have been aware that folks who are depressed need very specific suggestions and techniques — approaches that make sense, are easy to learn, and are effective. On the recommendation of a number of my patients, I have written this book to share the ideas from the class with you. I think you'll find that the book provides practical and effective solutions to help you cope with depression. A good place to begin is by taking a look at what "depression" really is.

It is true that all human beings will, at some points during their lives, experience significant feelings of sadness, grief, disappointment and despair. People care about things; we care about our families, our friends, our jobs, our pets. When we lose a loved one, when marriages fall apart, or when we lose our jobs, it is normal to feel sad and upset. Disappointments or tragedies will strike our hearts at some time or another. It is just as human to experience grief when there is a loss as it is to bleed when you have been cut. Often when people face painful life events, they will say that they feel "depressed." But it's important to note that feeling "sad" or "blue" does not necessarily mean that you are *depressed*.

Clinical depression differs from normal sadness in five basic ways:
- Depression is more intensely painful.
- Depression lasts longer.
- Depression interferes with normal day-to-day functioning.
- Depression is a destructive emotion (unlike grief, which is painful, but is an emotional experience that leads to healing).
- Depression typically is more than just a painful emotional feeling. Depression represents a syndrome (cluster of symptoms) often involving problems in social interaction, behavior, thinking and biological functioning.

Full-blown clinical depressions are not rare. One out of five people will experience a severe clinical depression at some point in their lives. In one out of fifteen, the depression will be so severe as to warrant hospitalization. The suicide rate for individuals experiencing *repeated major clinical depressions* is about fifteen percent. In some types of depression there are hormonal changes that occur which can profoundly interfere with the functioning of the immune system. The result is that the person is less able to ward off illness and is at higher risk for health problems.

While these may seem like gloomy statistics, there are two hopeful points I want to emphasize. First, is that *if you are depressed, you are not alone.* So many times people feel utterly alone in their suffering. Depression is a tremendously common human condition. However, like many emotional concerns and problems, many people feel inhibited or ashamed to reveal to others that they are or have been depressed. Many times there is a negative stigma attached to this condition. It is extremely unfortunate that this is the case. Suffice it to say that depression is very common and will touch the lives of almost every family.

The second positive point is that *there is help and hope.* Depression is one of the most treatable emotional conditions. This book will help you understand more about depression, give some guidelines to help you make decisions about treatment, teach you some effective skills for combating depression, and discuss professional treatment.

"I Feel Depressed"

It is common for people to be aware of that aspect of a physical illness that hurts the most or causes the most problems. These are the symptoms they report to the doctor. The same is true with depression. When someone says "I feel depressed," it may mean many different things. Here are a few common ways that people experience depression:

- Sadness, despair, sense of loss, emptiness, feeling blue (the kinds of feelings most people experience when a loved one dies);
- Apathy, indifference, low or no motivation, fatigue;
- Inability to experience excitement or pleasure, a loss of a zest for life;
- Increased sensitivity to criticism or rejection; feelings are easily hurt;
- Low self-esteem, lack of confidence, feeling inadequate;
- Irritability, easy frustration, anger;
- Guilty feelings, self-blame, self-hatred;
- Feelings of hopelessness and/or helplessness

Although these problems describe the most common aspects of depression, they represent only a few of the many symptoms that occur. Depression is a complex condition, and many people experience a combination of symptoms, not just an unpleasant feeling.

In the following chapter, we'll take a look the common *types* of depression. Different types of depression require different types of treatment. As you read this next section, please be thinking about yourself and taking stock of any particular problems or symptoms that you experience. Knowing this will make it easier to decide what kinds of treatment can be helpful.

2

All Depressions Are Not Alike

Depression affects people in many ways. The symptoms are often perplexing and worrisome. Many depressed people think they are going crazy or that they have a serious physical illness (even when their doctor finds no evidence of disease). By understanding the nature of your problem, in all likelihood you will feel less scared and less confused. And you will be in a position to make better informed choices about treatment. Depressions are not all alike, and treatments vary.

It is helpful to divide clinical depressions into three subtypes: *psychological depressions* (emotional reactions to losses and disappointments), *biological depressions* (depressions that in many respects are true medical illnesses), and a *mixed type* (a blend of emotional and physical reactions).

Psychological Depressions: Psychological depressions can be defined in two ways. First, they are triggered by psychological or emotional events. For example, a woman's husband announces that he is going to get a divorce and in response the woman becomes depressed. She can understand her feelings because it makes sense to her that she feels sad in response to the breakup of her marriage. In this example, there was a specific painful, stressful event (divorce). Many situational triggers for depression, however, may be more obscure or ill-defined. An example is the married man who has experienced a gradually-developing emotional distance in his marriage. His wife is more detached and less affectionate. This was not a sudden event, but represents a loss all the same. As often happens in such instances, he may become aware of "something missing" in his relationship, and this may trigger a depression. Thus the psychological or emotional trigger may be sudden and obvious or gradual and insidious. But there is a change in the life situation — relationships, lifestyle, or job — that acts as a trigger.

The second characteristic of a psychological depression is that the symptoms are exclusively psychological/emotional. In pure psychological depressions biological functioning is relatively unaffected.

Figure 2-A

Psychological Symptoms of Depression

- Sadness and despair
- Irritability
- Low self-esteem
- Apathy. No motivation
- Interpersonal problems
- Guilt feelings
- Negative thinking
- Suicidal thoughts

Mike is a good example of psychological depression. He had his heart set on a promotion, after two years on the job. He had worked hard, and felt he was doing well. Last month a position opened up, but another employee — one who had been with the company only six months — was given the job. It was tremendously upsetting for Mike to be passed over for the promotion. During the past few weeks he has felt preoccupied with feelings of inadequacy and low self-esteem. He often thinks to himself: "I'm never going to get a promotion. Obviously I just don't have what it takes." A part of his reaction to this event has been to progressively withdraw from life. He has turned down offers to go out to dinner. He prefers to go home at night, have a drink, and just go to bed. Most of the time he feels sad and "unmotivated." Every now and then, he entertains fleeting ideas about suicide.

Mike has experienced no major changes in his sleep, appetite, or sex drive. However, he has progressively intense feelings of sadness and low self-esteem, and is becoming socially withdrawn. His emotional reaction is in response to a life event and is characteristic of a psychological depression.

Biological Depressions: A second major category is biological depression, triggered by some type of physical (physiological) event, rather than a response to life changes or painful experiences. For this reason biological depressions seem to "come out of the blue" and often leave the affected person perplexed: "I can't understand why I feel so bad . . . Things have been fine in my life . . . It makes no sense." In addition to psychological or emotional symptoms, there are often a host of physical symptoms caused by chemical malfunctions in the nervous and hormonal systems (more on this in chapters 7 and 15).

Figure 2-B

Physical Symptoms of Depression

- Sleep disturbances
- Appetite disturbances
- Loss of sex drive
- Fatigue and decreased energy
- Inability to experience pleasure (Anhedonia)
- Family history of depression, suicide, eating disorders or alcoholism

---

Joel is a fifty-two-year-old lab technician, married with two grown children. He is considered to be an extremely hard-working man and is well liked. Last month, for no apparent reason, Joel started to experience some gradual changes. Although normally quite sociable, he began to feel uncomfortable being around people. He told his wife that he didn't know why, but would prefer to cancel their social engagements. ("I don't know why, I just don't feel up to it!") At work he seemed to withdraw and be especially quiet. Several people asked him if he was feeling sick. He said, "Yea, kinda."

At the same time, there were some changes in his physiological functioning. He started to notice that food just didn't taste right, and his appetite dropped off. In the past three weeks, he has lost four pounds. Also, he has started to wake up at 4:00 a.m. and is unable to return to sleep. This sleep pattern is quite unusual for Joel.

He finally consulted with his family doctor. He said "I just don't feel like myself . . . I feel kind of sad, but I don't know why. There's nothing going wrong in my life . . . everything's fine. Except me. I just feel tired all the time, and I don't want to be around anyone."

This picture is one which suggests a pure biological depression. It came "out of the blue." There were no identifiable stressful events or life changes. Also a part of the picture are gradually developing biological symptoms.

Bipolar disorder is a relatively common psychiatric illness which causes severe depression. This biological condition, also often referred to as manic-depressive illness, affects between 3.5 and 5 percent of the population. The symptoms include serious depressions alternating with episodes of mania (e.g., restlessness, agitation, increased energy, decreased need for sleep, impulsivity, and racing thoughts). There is substantial research evidence to indicate that bipolar disorder is a genetically-transmitted, biologically-based illness. We will discuss bipolar disorder in greater detail in chapter 17.

Psychological Depressions with Biological Symptoms (Mixed Type): This group represents a very large number of people experiencing clinical depression. Mixed type depression has a psychological trigger, but in these cases, the person experiences both emotional *and* physical symptoms.

Figure 2-C

Additional Symptoms that May Be Seen in
Both Psychological & Biological Depressions

- Poor concentration and poor recent memory
- Hypochondria: excessive concern with one's health
- Drug/Alcohol Abuse
- Excessive emotional sensitivity (including anger and irritability)
- Pronounced mood swings
- Anxiety

Eve is a thirty-two-year-old married woman who recently learned that her thirty-four-year-old husband has cancer. Since hearing this news two weeks ago, she has had periods of intense sadness and crying spells, frequent thoughts about his illness, and fears about being alone, should he die. She also is plagued with feelings of guilt and self-blame. She feels guilty for having taken him for granted during the past few years. In addition to these emotional symptoms, she also has had a noticeable loss of sexual desire and has what she describes as "terrible sleep," waking up a dozen times during each night. Eve's depressive reactions clearly are of the mixed type. She is responding to a significant, painful event, and part of the reaction involves biological symptoms.

The importance in making distinctions between the three types of depression has to do with treatment. There is convincing evidence that people suffering from biological and mixed type depressions tend to respond well to treatment with antidepressant medications (approximately seventy to eighty percent of *properly diagnosed* biological and mixed depression patients treated with antidepressant medications can show a good clinical response).

If you have a pure biological depression you may only require medication treatment and support. However, if you have a mixed type of depression, you may benefit from or need both medication treatment *and* other types of treatment such as individual counseling or psychotherapy and/or the self-help strategies outlined in this book. Finally, if you fit the description of a pure psychological depression, generally antidepressant medication treatments are not indicated, (although there are some exceptions to this). People with psychological depressions can benefit tremendously from certain types of psychotherapy and from the self-help strategies outlined in this book.

Single Episodes vs. Recurring Depression and Relapse

Some people experience only one episode of depression, recover, and never again go through a period of severe symptoms. Unfortunately, that pattern is the exception rather than the rule. Approximately two-thirds of major depressions are likely to recur. While some people function normally between episodes, many continue to experience persistent, low-grade depressive symptoms.

As we begin to explore diagnosis and treatment of your depression, there are two primary goals to keep in mind: (1) *Do everything possible to resolve the current depression;* and (2) *Take steps to avoid a relapse.*

The strategies described in later chapters are proven effective, and can help you achieve both goals. Self-help approaches are discussed in chapters 11, 12, and 13; professional psychotherapy in chapter 14; and medication in chapter 15 and 17.

While some individuals with a history of frequent depressive episodes may take antidepressants regularly to avoid relapse, the more common strategy is to resolve the current depression first, then stay alert for any early sign of relapse. If and when symptoms begin to surface, a prompt re-start of medication can often "nip it in the bud."

But how do you know if you really have "depression"? And, if so, what type? Most important, what can you *do* about it? Keep reading . . .

3

Understanding the Symptoms
of Depression

The previous chapter presented an overview of the symptoms of psychological, biological, and mixed-type depressions. Now we'll take a more detailed look at those symptoms. This chapter should help you better understand yourself and any of these symptoms that you may be experiencing. By understanding the nature of your problems, you will be better able to make good choices about possible treatment.

Psychological Symptoms of Depression

• *Sadness and Despair:* Often these are the symptoms of depression that hurt the most and are most noticeable. Other related feelings may include feelings of emptiness, disappointment, gloom, feeling "down" or "blue." Heaviness — especially in the pit of the stomach — and literal "heartache" are physical aspects of this symptom. About forty percent of people experiencing serious depression do not really feel sad. Rather, the primary change in mood is to begin feeling very irritable and easily frustrated. In such cases, even very minor problems or frustrations may feel overwhelming and may lead to outbursts of temper and irritability. Many people suffering from depression do not feel especially sad or depressed, but when asked "Are you happy?" The answer clearly is "No."

• *Low Self-Esteem* includes feelings of worthlessness, inadequacy, lack of self-confidence, and self-hatred. "I can't do it," "I'm no good," and "I never do anything right" are examples of self-talk which are common among people with low self-esteem. These folks have often grown up unable to please themselves, their parents, their teachers.

They have often experienced failures in school, in relationships, in sports, and on the job.

They typically value other people above themselves, and usually defer to others' opinions and guidance. Sometimes the feelings are temporary — perhaps in relation to losing a job or relationship — but often they are a lifelong burden.

• *Apathy* is the lack of motivation to do things, social withdrawal, decreased level of activity, and/or restriction of life activities. This symptom can, in itself, lead to more serious problems in a sort of depressive vicious cycle. For instance, feeling apathetic could lead you to conclude, "What's the use, I just don't feel like going out and being with others." Yet failure to engage in social or recreational activities eventually leads to life's becoming more and more void of enjoyable, meaningful activities. A life relatively empty of pleasure is felt by some researchers to be a major cause of depression (see Lewinsohn and Graf, 1973, listed in the "References" section at the end of this book). Also decreased activity itself leads to physical changes, like fatigue and constipation, which cause additional discomfort.

• *Interpersonal Problems:* When people are depressed, they often become especially sensitive to criticism or rejection. They may feel uncomfortable or inadequate around other people, or experience increased feelings of loneliness. Depressed people may not feel "Okay" about being assertive (i.e., it may be hard to stand up for yourself, to voice your opinions, feelings or beliefs, to ask others for help or support, or to say "no"). Many people have these problems when they are not depressed, but such concerns become more intense during depression. Also, some people are relatively at ease with others most of the time, and notice these problems only when depressed. One depressed man told me, "I usually feel fine when talking with others but lately I've lost confidence in myself. I worry about how I'm coming across, I feel inhibited about saying what I really think or feel. I feel as if there is something wrong with me."

• *Guilt Feelings:* It is normal and appropriate to experience feelings of regret or remorse when you make a mistake or inadvertently hurt someone. However as Dr. David Burns has pointed out, guilt is a feeling that contains not only regret or remorse, but also a belief that "I am a bad person." (Burns, 1980, pp. 178-204). It is this belief in a "badness of self" that makes guilt a painful and destructive emotion.

• ***Negative Thinking:*** The term "cognitive distortions" is used by psychologists to refer to a tendency to think in negative and pessimistic ways. (Cognitions are thoughts and perceptions.) Distortions or errors in thinking and perceiving are seen in almost all types of depression. As a person begins to feel depressed, thoughts and perceptions become extremely negative and pessimistic. Such distortions not only are a *symptom* of depression but also are a major *cause* of depression, and in fact are probably the most potent factor that prolongs and intensifies depression. I'll be talking a good deal more about negative thinking in chapters 11 and 12.

• ***Suicidal Thoughts:*** Thoughts about suicide are extremely common in depression. Although most people who think about suicide do not commit suicide, nevertheless, suicidal ideas must always be taken seriously. Most of the time, suicidal ideas reflect a view of the future which is colored by excessive pessimism and a sense of hopelessness.

Biological Symptoms of Depression

The following symptoms occur because of significant biochemical changes that take place in the nervous and hormonal systems (see chapters 17 and 15 for details). The presence of one or more of these symptoms should serve as a signal that there is a biological malfunction accounting for at least part of your symptoms.

• ***Sleep Disturbances:*** A number of changes can take place in the natural sleep cycle. *Difficulty falling asleep* (initial insomnia) is a common symptom of stress in general. Even minor stresses can cause most individuals problems in falling asleep. It has been estimated that at any one given time, thirty-five percent of people are experiencing some difficulty in falling asleep. However, several sleep problems are rather unique to depression and reflect a malfunction in that part of the brain that regulates sleep cycles. Depression-related sleep disturbances include: *Early Morning Awakening:* Waking up two or more hours before you would normally awaken, and being unable to return to sleep. *Middle Insomnia:* Waking up frequently during the night, but generally able to go back to sleep. Often the result is that you may have slept, but feel as if you did not. During the following day, you feel exhausted. *Hypersomnia:* Excessive oversleeping. *Poor Quality Sleep:* At times you may be able to sleep eight or more hours, but during the day feel fatigued and exhausted. One effect depression can have is to reduce the amount of time you spend in the deep sleep that ordinarily restores a person physically and emotionally.

It has been found that the severe sleep problems seen in depression are likely due to the direct effects of increased stress hormones that accompany depression.

• ***Appetite Disturbances:*** Excessive increase in or loss of appetite with a corresponding weight gain or loss. Generally appetite loss is considered to be more indicative of biological depression. Appetite increase *may* be a psychological response because eating often is a form of self-soothing and can temporarily reduce an inner sense of emptiness. Some types of biological depression may, however, be present with increased appetite.

• ***Loss of Sex Drive*** represents a biologically-based reduction in sex drive or interest. Certainly there are many psychological causes for sexual problems. If there are serious marital problems, the partner in the relationship may become disinterested because of lack of love or trust. The decreased sex drive that is seen in biological depressions occurs on a purely physical basis and may be seen in people who have happy, loving relationships. One depressed lady said, "I honestly love my husband. I want so badly to feel sexually turned on by him, but it just doesn't happen, and I'm worried that he'll think I don't care about him." Often this decrease in sexual interest is misunderstood by the spouse and becomes a source of conflict.

• ***Fatigue and Decreased Energy:*** Many depressed people report "I feel totally exhausted . . . it's like I have to drag myself through the day. And sleeping doesn't help. If I take a nap I usually feel even more tired when I wake up." This can be a primary symptom or secondary to a sleep disturbance.

• ***Inability to Experience Pleasure:*** Psychologists call this "Anhedonia," and it is often experienced as a loss of a zest for life. A mild degree of anhedonia may be seen in psychological depressions, but if pronounced, it's likely to reflect a chemical malfunction in certain parts of the nervous system that operate as pleasure centers.

• ***Hormonal Changes:*** Often severe depressions result in marked changes in hormones. Most notable are decreases in *growth hormone,* which can contribute to osteoporosis, and elevations in *cortisol,* which may be a factor in the increased risk of heart disease in chronically depressed people.

• ***Family History of Depression, Suicide, Alcoholism or Eating Disorders:*** While not a "symptom" of depression, family history is still a very important marker for biological depression and an important issue mental health professionals consider when evaluating their patients for medication or other treatment. Biological depression tends to run in families. Alcoholism, suicide and eating disorders such as anorexia nervosa or bulimia may share a similar underlying biological basis. Thus, if your parent or several blood relatives experienced these problems, there is increased risk that you may have some genetic vulnerability. This does not by any means indicate that the child of a depressed parent absolutely will become depressed, but there is an increased risk.

Additional Symptoms of Psychological, Biological and Mixed-Type Depressions

• *Poor Concentration and Poor Recent Memory (Forgetfulness):* Many people seen in mental health clinics are fearful that they have brain tumors or Alzheimer's Disease. Often they are experiencing forgetfulness and poor concentration due to depression. Depression and stress are the most common causes for poor memory and concentration difficulties. Again certain diseases can also cause these symptoms. Be sure to be evaluated by a physician if such symptoms occur.

• *Hypochondria:* One of the most common causes for hypochondria (excessive worry about one's health in the face of evidence from a physical examination that no disease is present) is an underlying and often unrecognized depression.

• *Drug/Alcohol Abuse:* Many instances of drug and/or alcohol abuse represent attempts to soothe the pain of depression. Alcohol abuse, itself, can also cause severe depressions.

• *Excessive Emotional Sensitivity:* An overwhelming, intense surge of feelings (e.g., tearfulness, irritability, etc.) in response to minor frustrations.

• *Pronounced Mood Swings:* Occasionally people experience severe mood swings, vacillating from depression to inappropriate euphoria (often referred to as mania or hypo-mania). Such mood swings may be associated with a type of biological depression called "Bipolar Illness," a condition previously referred to as Manic-Depressive Illness." (See chapter 17).

• *Anxiety:* About sixty percent of depressed people also suffer considerable anxiety (tension, nervousness, worry, agitation, fretting). Anxiety can be almost continuous or can come in the form of sudden explosions, referred to as "panic attacks."

• *Panic Attacks:* These are very sudden, intense episodes of severe physical and emotional distress that are characterized by some or all of the following signs and symptoms: rapid heart rate, shortness of breath, faintness, dizziness, tingling in the fingers and toes, sometimes chest pains, a sense of danger or impending doom (although often without knowing what one is afraid of), panicky feelings and an intense fear of going crazy or loss of control. The episodes generally last only five to ten minutes. Such an attack many times is not triggered by a specific stressful event, but rather "comes out of the blue." Panic attacks can occur in people who are not depressed, but approximately fifty percent of people with panic disorder are also depressed. It should be noted that some medical conditions can cause similar symptoms, and any individual with panic symptoms should be seen by a physician first to rule out other conditions.

Depression Across the Life Span

Depression certainly can occur in children and teenagers (the yearly prevalence rate for serious depression in young children is 3 percent and 10 percent in teenagers). These depressions are often harder to spot, because most depressed kids are not sad! The most typical symptoms of depression in children and teens are *anhedonia* and *irritability.* Anhedonia (inability to experience pleasure) can become all consuming, and most depressed children show a marked withdrawal from life. They pull away from friends, stay alone in their rooms, and generally appear to be devitalized, bored, fatigued, and uninvolved. They may also suffer from many of the other symptoms of depression (see Figure 3-A). Suicides among teens have increased 600 percent from 1950 to 2000! *Depression in young people must be treated.*

Figure 3-A

Symptoms of Depression in Children and Adolescents

- Loss of interest in life activities (anhedonia)
- Irritability
- Social withdrawal
- Sleep problems
- Academic problems
- Vague physical complaints (e.g. headaches, stomach aches)

Elderly people also become depressed (although it is important to emphasize that major depression is not a normal part of aging). One particular depressive symptom that can become especially pronounced in older people is memory impairment. This at times may be misdiagnosed as a sign of dementia (e.g., Alzheimer's disease). If depression is the cause, it certainly can be successfully treated.

It is important to determine the type of depression you are experiencing so you can make good decisions regarding treatment. A tremendous number of people are seriously depressed and do not receive treatment. Also, a very large number of people are treated, but treated inappropriately (see chapter 14). I think that it is important for you to understand as much as you can about depression and the problems you are encountering, and to seek out and insist on receiving appropriate treatment. This is your right.

4

Diagnosing Yourself
and Monitoring Your Recovery

Now that you are familiar with the major signs and symptoms of depression it will be helpful to complete the self-diagnosis checklist on pages 24-26.

The checklist can be used for three purposes: 1) to help you determine just how depressed you really are; 2) to self-diagnose your possible need for medication treatment; and most importantly, 3) as a way to monitor change over time. In most instances, as a person begins to recover from depression there are positive changes in symptoms, and yet these important signs of improvement may go unnoticed by the depressed person. Friends, family members and therapists often see signs of recovery long before the depressed person becomes aware of such changes. This is probably because in the early stages of recovery there still exists a tendency to view oneself and the world in a very negative way. The use of this checklist can help.

Susan had been quite depressed and in treatment for four weeks. She had filled out this checklist during her first visit. When I saw her for the fourth time, she stated, "I still feel depressed . . . things are no better." However, from my perspective she "looked" much less depressed, more alive and spontaneous, more energetic. She was still quite sad, but there were changes that showed outwardly. I asked her to fill out the checklist again and when she had completed it, we compared it to the one she had done during the first visit. There were positive changes in the areas of sleep, energy level and emotional control. When she reviewed both checklists, she said, "Well, now that I think about this, things are better. In some ways I still feel very crummy, but there *have* been changes.

"This kind of response frequently occurs. It will be helpful for you to use this checklist as a yardstick to measure your improvement. For Susan, this exercise helped her to see that she was making some important gains, which increased her sense of hope. Restoring a sense of realistic hope is, in itself, a powerful antidote to pessimistic and depressive feelings.

I urge you to complete the checklist now and, to monitor your changes, at the end of each week during the initial stages of your recovery from depression.

Depression Checklist

I. Biological Functioning   Scores

A. Sleep Problems
    1. No sleep problems   0
    2. Occasional sleep problems   1
    3. Frequent awakenings during the night or early morning
       awakening
         a. 1-3 times during last week   2
         b. 4 or more times during last week   3

B. Appetite Problems
    1. No changes in appetite   0
    2. Some appetite change (up or down)
       but no weight gain or loss   1
    3. Significant appetite change (up or down)
       with weight gain or loss (3 lbs. plus or minus
       during past month)   3

C. Fatigue
    1. Little or no noticeable daytime fatigue   0
    2. Fatigued or exhausted during the day
         a. occasionally   1
         b. 1-3 days during last week   2
         c. 4 or more days during last week   3

D. Sex Drive
    1. No change in sex drive   0
    2. Decrease in sex drive
        a. slight   1
        b. moderate   2
        c. no sex drive   3

E. Anhedonia
    1. Despite times of sadness, I am able to
       have times of enjoyment or pleasure   0
    2. Decreased ability to enjoy life
        a. slight   1
        b. moderate   2
        c. absolutely no joy or sense of aliveness   3

TOTAL SCORE: BIOLOGICAL FUNCTIONING   [ ]

II. Emotional/Psychological Symptoms
A. Sadness and Despair
    1. No pronounced sadness   0
    2. Occasional sadness   1
    3. Times of intense sadness   2
    4. Intense sadness almost every day   3

B. Self-Esteem
    1. I feel confident and good about myself   0
    2. I sometimes doubt myself   1
    3. I often feel inadequate, inferior or
       lacking in self-confidence   2
    4. I feel completely worthless most of the time   3

C. Apathy and Motivation
    1. It is easy to feel motivated and enthusiastic about things   0
    2. I occasionally find it hard to "get started"
       on projects, work, etc.   1
    3. I often feel unmotivated or apathetic   2
    4. It is almost impossible to "get started"
       with projects, work, etc.   3

D. Negative Thinking/Pessimism
    1. I think in relatively positive ways about
       my life and my future   0
    2. I occasionally feel pessimistic   1
    3. I often feel pessimistic   2
    4 The world seems extremely negative to me;
       the future looks hopeless   3

E. Emotional Control
    1. When I feel unpleasant feelings such emotions
       may hurt, but I do not feel totally overwhelmed   1
    2. I occasionally feel overwhelmed by inner emotions   2
    3. I often feel extremely overwhelmed by inner
       feelings *or* I feel absolutely no inner feelings   3

F. Irritability and Frustration
    1. I do not experience undue irritability and frustration   0
    2. I occasionally feel quite irritable and frustrated   1
    3. I often feel quite irritable and become easily frustrated
       a. 1-3 days during the last week   2
       b. 4+ days during the last week   3

TOTAL SCORE:
EMOTIONAL/PSYCHOLOGICAL SYMPTOMS   [ ]

Computing Your Score and Interpreting the Results:
Let's take a look at the results. A total score can be computed for the "Biological Functioning" and "Emotional/Psychological Symptoms" sections of the checklist. To compute your score, add up your response to each symptom, entering the total score in the box at the bottom of each page.

    Biological Functioning: Responses of 2 or 3 on *any* of the items A-E may suggest that your biological functioning has been affected by the depression and that antidepressant medication treatment may be indicated (especially if any scores of 3 are present). If this is the case, it will be important to consult with a psychiatrist, your family physician or a mental health therapist regarding medical treatment. If all scores are 0 or 1, antidepressant medications probably are not indicated. *Interpretation of the total Score:*0-5 Mild, 6-10 Moderate, 11-15 Severe Biological Depression.

Emotional/Psychological Symptoms: Responses of 2 or 3 on any suggest psychological depression. *Interpretation of the total score:* 0-5 Mild, 6-10 Moderate, 11-18 Severe Psychological Symptoms. High scores on both Biological and Emotional/Psychological sections indicate a mixed type of depression. As mentioned earlier, such depressive reactions often can be helped with medications.

Please continue to complete this short checklist at the end of each week to monitor your progress as well as psychotherapy.

In the next few chapters, we'll take a look at what causes depression. Part Two of the book will help you find out what *you* can do to overcome your depression and how to get professional help if you need it.

5

What Causes Depression? — Personal History

"I must be going crazy. What's the matter with me? I feel so awful. I can't think, I have no energy, no motivation. Why am I feeling so bad?!"

The pain of depression is often amplified by a sense of confusion and perplexity. At times, it may be very easy to understand why you're feeling depressed. As one of my patients said, "Of course I feel depressed. My wife left me, I'm alone, my whole life has been turned upside-down. People get depressed when they are going through a divorce. Right?"

True, but often the causes are hidden or obscure. Many times people feel that depression comes "out of the blue." One reason it's important to understand what causes depression is that understanding can help you make better decisions about treatment. Just as it is true that not all sore throats respond to antibiotics, in a similar fashion, not all depressions respond to the same treatment. Once you know for sure that you have strep throat, antibiotics are the treatment of choice. Likewise, knowing what causes your depression is necessary for deciding upon the most effective types of treatment.

Another reason for uncovering the causes of your depression is that it can be tremendously helpful for you to make sense out of what otherwise is a perplexing condition. Understanding "why" can decrease that sense of confusion and mystery that surrounds depression. Such understanding can improve your chances for recovery.

In this chapter, I would like briefly to discuss some of the major causes of depression. Please keep in mind, of course, that it is often a combination of factors which eventually leads to depression. (This chapter's emphasis will be on how life history contributes to depression. Later chapters will deal with current events and biological factors.)

Early Life Experiences

Assume for a minute that two people are going to be in a race in which they must run barefoot across a gravel parking lot. Further assume that one of the racers already has blisters on his feet before the race begins. The race may be painful for both, but the person with pre-existing injuries will experience a lot more pain. In a similar fashion, it has been shown that a number of emotionally damaging early life experiences can set the stage for greatly increased risk of depression in adult life. Certainly, having experienced such early painful events is not a guarantee that a person will inevitably become depressed later on. However, some experiences greatly increase vulnerability to depression. Such early circumstances as those described in the next few pages help explain why, when two people are exposed to the exact same stressful condition, one person may feel bad but cope well, while the other becomes depressed.

• *Early Neglect:* Recent studies have shown that significant early neglect can result in abnormal brain development (in particular a defect in the hypothalamus which results in chronic over-secretion of the brain chemical, *cortico-tropin releasing factor*). When this occurs (especially during the first few months of life) the result can be a permanent change in brain functioning that lasts even if later life circumstances greatly improve. The behavioral consequence of this is an increased vulnerability to depression. Knowledge of this effect has led to an increasing appreciation of the important role of holding, touching, and rocking of infants and young children.

• *Early Losses:* Young children are especially sensitive to the loss of loved ones. It is a normal part of development to establish strong bonds, especially with one's parents. A parent may be lost through death, divorce or marital separation, jobs which require the parent to be gone for prolonged periods of time, and serious illness requiring long periods of hospitalization. Many "lost" parents may actually be *present,* yet emotionally detached or uninvolved. A very ill, bed-ridden parent, for instance, may love his child and yet be quite unavailable emotionally.

Children raised by depressed parents often go on to become depressed adults. That parent may have dearly loved the child, but in a powerful way the depression took away the parent's energy and ability to be meaningfully involved with the child.

At times, a child is unwanted and unloved, or extremely stressful family circumstances result in parental harshness or rejection. Children of alcoholics commonly experience very significant emotional deprivation. Prolonged alcohol abuse often has a devastating effect on parents, and can interfere with the parents' basic capacity to form intimate bonds with their children. Many adult children of alcoholics suffer the effects of this early loss of emotional involvement with their parents.

Thus there are many ways a child can experience a sense of profound loss early in life. These losses often result in three main problems that might continue throughout adult life:

Difficulties with intimacy: To become attached to and then to lose a parent can cause a child to become extremely cautious about getting emotionally close to anyone again. Such children may inwardly long for closeness, but harbor deep fears of rejection and loss and thus never allow themselves to feel truly close again. This inner sense of longing for love and emotional isolation can increase the likelihood of depression.

Anxiety and fear: Children need to have parents to provide a sense of basic safety and security in the world. Losses often leave children feeling quite insecure and afraid.

Profound sadness and grief: It is remarkable how fears of intimacy, insecurity, or sadness can continue deep inside a person years and years after the grievous event occurred. Such children are at very high risk for developing strong reactions to losses experienced later in life. When this happens, the present day loss touches on deep, unhealed wounds from the past. It may be hard to understand why a person reacts so strongly to a loss until one stops to consider such childhood experiences.

Linda is a twenty-seven-year-old, single woman who became extremely embarrassed while telling me that she had felt very depressed since her pet cat, Callie, died three weeks earlier. "I feel so stupid. People feel sad when their pets die, but I've been totally falling apart since Callie died." Her friends could not understand how the death of a cat could provoke such strong, painful feelings. In talking with Linda, the reason soon became clear. When Linda was young, her mother had become mentally ill; she was repeatedly hospitalized throughout Linda's childhood. Apparently, her father was so unable or unwilling to cope with raising Linda and her two brothers that he placed them in a receiving home (she called it an orphanage) for several months each time her mother went into the hospital. "The first time my Dad came to visit us, I cried so hard that it upset him and he said he couldn't stand to see me cry. So he wouldn't even come to visit us at all!" Linda learned how not ever to cry, even if intensely sad, for fear of upsetting her father. She experienced tremendous sadness during these times in the "orphanage," but learned to hide her inner feelings. Later, as a teenager and young adult, she was so afraid to get attached to someone that she kept at a distance and rarely dated. Yet her inner needs for love and closeness did not disappear. She let herself express fondness and nurturance towards Callie. Callie's death caused her both to react to the loss of her beloved pet *and* to recall terribly painful feelings buried inside of her since childhood. It was important for Linda to come to understand the reasons for her strong reaction. After a few sessions of psychotherapy and much discussion about her childhood experiences, she commented to me, "My feelings make more sense to me now. It still hurts a lot, but my feelings don't seem so weird or abnormal now. I understand why I am hurting so much."

Fortunately, early losses do not absolutely guarantee that a person will become depressed as an adult. Two important factors can help a child live through painful losses: first, the emotional availability of at least one other adult. It is not unusual that the other parent, or a grandmother or an aunt may make *the* crucial difference for a child who has lost a parent. Second, it is very important to help children grieve. Had Linda's father been available, had he kept the children at home, or at least had he let her cry, her life would have been different. Giving the child a message, "This is hard; It's okay to cry," and sharing your own tears and pain with the child can help prevent emotional wounds that can last a lifetime.

• *Pervasively Harsh Atmosphere:* All parents, from time to time, lose their tempers; all parents occasionally are insensitive; all parents make mistakes that hurt their children. But occasional mistakes do not leave deep wounds. In fact, many child development specialists believe that you need only provide a "good enough" atmosphere, and most kids thrive and grow; "good enough" being where the majority of experiences are positive or even neutral — where the good outweighs the bad. After all, nobody's perfect!

In contrast to this, however, is the pervasively harsh atmosphere found in all too many homes. Sometimes physical abuse is a part of the picture, but basically I am talking about an overriding attitude expressed towards the child: "You are worthless, you are not wanted, you are stupid and inadequate." I recently saw a father in the local grocery store shake his son and say, "You're just a little piece of shit." This is a profoundly damaging message to this boy, belittling and dehumanizing. It undercuts his basic worth as a person. On a day-to-day basis, these messages sink in. The child almost invariably comes to believe that the message — coming from one of the most important people in its life — is true. Such kids grow up with a damaged sense of self-worth. Even small failures or setbacks as adults touch on the inner painful belief. As one of my patients said, "Yeah, it's like when I screwed up at work and my boss chewed me out, I was thinking, he's right, I'm worthless. I've always been worthless, and always will be."

Failure, disappointments, and setbacks are inevitable aspects of adult life. Under the best of circumstances life is often hard. Growing up in an emotionally harsh atmosphere increases the pain of later stresses and leaves a lasting mark on the spirit of the child.

• *Lack of Support for Growth:* Children need protection and nurturing, but they also need encouragement to grow. An inherent inner drive in everyone is the urge to grow up, become yourself, have an opinion, take action, assert yourself, and make a mark on the world. At times, parents do not support growth. This can happen in several ways. First, some parents want to hang on to their babies. It's hard to give up the closeness and warmth that an infant can provide. When the young child starts to pull away, responding to an inner innate desire to thrust out into the world on his own, a parent may feel hurt, upset, or rejected. One way growth and autonomy are undermined is for the parent to continue to perceive the child as helpless and to do everything for the child. It may be hard for such a parent to see her child make mistakes. For example, as the toddler starts to walk, the parent may feel the urge to "rescue" the child each time he starts to fall. The result may appear to be that the child is protected from hurt. At a deeper level, the child is given the message "I see you as helpless. I don't think you can do it on your own. I don't have confidence in your ability, so I will protect you or do things for you." Often parents underestimate the profound effect this has on a child. Should such a pattern continue, the result is that the child grows up believing: "I can't do things. I don't have confidence in myself." This can leave the child on shaky ground, afraid to try new things. Such people may grow up needing constant help from others, believing that "I can't do it on my own." As an adult, the pain of losing a spouse or parent can become very intense if, inwardly, one believes "I can't function without them." A part of the reaction, thus, is not only normal sadness and loss, but also a marked loss of self-confidence.

A second affront to growth is when a child starts to do things independently and parents respond to the child's behavior with ridicule or belittling. One of my patients told me that he remembers making a toy plane with some wood and a few nails. He wanted to do woodwork like his Dad. He took in the finished product to show his father and his father laughed at him and even held up the little plane, showing it to his friends and making a belittling, sarcastic remark. "I was so humiliated, I never tried making anything again." Parents need to support these early thrusts towards autonomy and self-expression.

In some families children are subjected to perfectionistic demands. A child may do her best, but "it isn't good enough." Straight A's earn the parent comment, "Why weren't they A-pluses?" Again, as the child is moving toward self-expression, the message is "Your work isn't good enough." These messages sink in and form the core of later feelings of low self-esteem.

For people experiencing lack of support for growth as children, later life experiences (especially failures) strike deep, painful chords. Kids growing up with adequate support develop a basic inner sense of "I'm okay." Later failures may sting, but are not devastating.

• *Child Abuse and Molestation:* The emotional trauma of physical and sexual abuse is profound. Such treatment, especially by parents, damages a child in a number of ways. Children count on parents to provide a sense of stability, trust, and security. Many researchers in the field of child abuse agree that one effect of abuse or molestation by parents is a dramatic erosion of basic feelings of security and safety. Also many, if not most, victims of abuse — especially sexual molestation — feel that they are to blame; at some level they come to believe: "It was my fault, I'm bad, dirty, disgusting." Again, this experience can sink into the core of a person's basic sense of self-worth.

It is clear that a number of early-life experiences have very significant consequences for development and later adjustment. Most children do not simply "outgrow" these painful early experiences. When they are ready to run the race of adult life, there are already deep and painful wounds to overcome.

6

What Causes Depression?
— Current Life Events

arly childhood traumas certainly make it more likely that a person✓ will become depressed. However, depression can strike even without such predisposing risk factors. No one is immune. Depression affects people from all walks of life and has little regard for social status, intelligence, or success in the world. Although some biological depressions come "out of the blue," most depressions represent reaction to life changes. Not all life changes result in depression, of course, but there are a number of common stressors that may kindle its onset.

Current or Recent Triggers for Depression

• Interpersonal Losses: Probably the number one trigger for depression, loss of a loved one, can be due to a number of life events: death, marital separation and divorce, children moving away from home, being rejected by a friend or lover. Such losses are not uncommon human experiences. In the United States each year, approximately 1,000,000 divorces are final, 8,000,000 people lose a loved one to death, and 800,000 of us become widows and widowers (Osterweis, M., et al. 1984). At any given time in the United States, there are 11,000,000 widows and 2,000,000 widowers. People frequently move away from friends to take new jobs, and millions of relationships with relatives and friends are destroyed by conflict.

Losses typically result in grief — a painful experience, but one that eventually leads to emotional recovery for most of us.

However, as many as thirty-five percent of people experiencing significant losses will become clinically depressed.

One of many misconceptions about "normal grieving" is the expectation that people should "get over" a death or divorce in a few months. Studies of emotional loss show that the period of normal grief is often much longer than most people suspect. It is helpful to think about three phases to the grieving process:

Phase 1: Initial shock, which may involve numbness, intense grieving, or a vacillation between emotional pain and numbness. — Phase 2: The grieving period per se, during which there are frequent periods of intense sadness and loneliness and the person may feel that "life is totally different." (This period of normal grief, contrary to popular belief, is long — generally two years for death of parent, four years for marital separation/divorce, four to six years for death of spouse, and eight to ten years for death of a child. Of course, the period may vary tremendously from person to person.) — Phase 3: Eventual resolution. Even with "resolution," however, the griever is *not* "over it." In fact, most people will continue to have times of painful remembering for years to come. Yet resolution may be assumed when the intensely painful surges of sadness have subsided or are much less frequent, and life feels "normal" again.

Anyone who has experienced a serious loss will tell you, "You never really get over it." Thankfully, however, hearts can heal; it just takes a long time. It is important to realize that grieving is a long and painful process, but not a sign of pathology or mental illness. In chapter 10, we'll take a closer look at the differences between grief and depression.

• *Existential Losses:* Robert just heard that a co-worker died of a heart attack while playing golf. The friend was only forty-eight years old. When I spoke to Robert, he said, "What upset me most was that it could have been me. It made me think about my life. It made me wonder, am I really happy? Is my life meaningful?" Often such losses force us to face very difficult questions about the meaning of our lives, our mortality, our basic satisfaction with life. It may be that much of what is behind the so-called "middle-age crisis" is a sort of depression triggered by these kinds of existential issues.

One of the main existential concerns that people commonly encounter is disillusionment or loss of a dream. Most of us have hopes and dreams, some well known to us, some mostly unconscious. Such dreams include

"I hope to have a family or a marriage that will fulfill me," or "I hope to find success and happiness in my job." Many times the reality of a job or a relationship does not match what one longs for inwardly. It is not unusual for a person to, in a sense, wake up one day and be struck with the painful awareness that "I'm not happy" in a relationship or a job.

People often go to great lengths to maintain hope even in the face of disappointing realities. Thirty-eight-old Pam told me: "It's been there for eleven years, every day. My husband doesn't care about me. He's treated me like trash, ignored me. Sometimes he's abusive. But I kept hoping he'd change. I kept saying that all we needed to do is to try a little harder. It's just now hitting me. He hasn't changed and he won't ever change. How could I have been so stupid?" She was not stupid; she was hopeful. Hope can be a bridge that helps people get over painful or difficult times. It can also blind people. Pam was able to ward off more painful feelings of loss by maintaining hope, but at some point the bubble popped. It was the eventual awareness of her profound disappointment that triggered a depression. Her dream of happiness in marriage was destroyed. This type of trigger for depression is just as real and powerful as other losses, but often not fully appreciated. Pam's friends made comments such as, "I don't see how come you're so upset. You've known about how he is for years." When she heard this, she felt bad. Her friends may have had good intentions, but were being critical. It does not matter how long she had lived with her husband's abuse. When her "illusion" of hope disappeared, she began to get depressed.

A second major type of existential loss is the recognition that, "I won't live forever." A twenty-year-old college student knows that this statement is true, but probably does not think about it much. But a forty-year-old person may look at this truth very differently. The death of parents or a friend their age often has a powerful way of forcing people to face their own mortality. And, as Rabbi Harold Kushner has said, "It is not the fear of death, of our lives ending, that haunts our sleep so much as the fear that our lives will not have mattered . . ." (1986, p. 20). This acute awareness of "time running out" may provoke not only worries about the future, but also grief about a life that has been empty, disappointing, or lacking in meaningfulness.

Society recognizes deaths and divorce as "legitimate" reasons for grief and depression. Existential issues, however, often are seen in a different light. A woman patient said to me after the death of her husband, "Oh, these things happen. It's just a part of growing old and you've gotta accept it." She was trying to convince me (and herself) that "these things happen," and that she should be able to cope with it. The reality was that she was suffering tremendously from the loss of her husband and her own awareness of her mortality. Her friends and family were sympathetic toward her regarding her husband's death. But they did not openly understand and support her fears and sadness as she faced the painful awareness of "her own" life coming to an end. Somehow, the death of her husband was a more acceptable loss; her existential crisis was minimized. As a result, she felt even more alone with her pain. Existential losses must be understood as very real and powerful causes for human suffering.

• ***Events that Lower Self-Esteem:*** Many life events may deal a blow to one's sense of esteem or self-worth. Personal failures (such as failing to receive a promotion), personal rejections and criticisms, and making mistakes are but a few of the many events that can lead to low self-esteem.

Andy, a forty-three-year-old bookkeeper, accidentally set his kitchen on fire. His house was saved, but there was extensive damage to the kitchen. Even though his insurance paid for the repair costs, for many months he felt a terrible, inner sense of self-loathing. "What was wrong with me? I was so stupid. I can't believe that I could have been so dumb." He suffered this initial loss, but for months was unable to forgive himself for making a mistake.

Carl had worked for twenty-three years for a machine shop. The business was sold and the new owner did not retain Carl on the staff despite an excellent work history. For two years, he was unable to find a job in his usual craft. He was also subject to ridicule and cruel jokes from a brother-in-law who took every opportunity to point out Carl's "chronic unemployment." These experiences caused Carl tremendous inner suffering and feelings of worthlessness.

Every human being has a need to feel a basic sense of self-worth; events such as those mentioned above often lead to depression.

• ***Physical Disease and Chronic Pain:*** Illnesses can create serious emotional distress. In some instances, a physical disease results in intense, daily pain, diminishing the quality of life and making it hard to experience moments of joy.

Some life-threatening and degenerative illnesses carry the specter of increasing disability and possibly death. One study evaluated a group of patients who suffered from spinal cord injuries, and another group which had muscular dystrophy. In both groups the degree of current disability was similar. However, spinal cord injury is generally a static condition: it does not get worse. With muscular dystrophy, there is continual deterioration. The degree of depression in the muscular dystrophy group was significantly higher than that of the spinal cord injury patients (Duveneck, et al. 1986). It is human nature to look toward the future, and many diseases unfortunately have a poor prognosis.

Some illnesses can result in physical limitations that dramatically alter one's life style. Sharon is a thirty-four-year-old woman whose passion in life is modern dance. She used to work as a secretary, living for the end of the day when she could leave and go to her dance classes. Two years ago, she developed severe crippling rheumatoid arthritis and had to completely give up dancing. "My whole life has changed. It feels empty now." Physical illnesses not only result in pain and sometimes fear of an uncertain future, but also may change a person's life in ways which result in depression.

Chronic pain often ultimately can lead to depression. This is due to the stress of the pain itself. Additionally, people suffering from chronic pain typically develop severely disturbed sleep. Long-term sleeping problems often either cause depression or make it worse.

• *Our Stressful New World:* 21st century technology exposes all of us to new sources of stress, including fears of terrorism and round-the-clock exposure to disasters and human suffering, via virtually instant media coverage around the globe. Some psychologists hypothesize that a common way people cope with living in a world full of heartache and tragedy is to maintain a fairly high level of denial and inattention. Many people have found it possible to maintain a long arm's length between themselves and many of the horrors of life (war, starvation, terrorism, racial discrimination, etc.). In this new world of technology and in-your-face media coverage, however, people are now exposed to an increasing amount of disturbing information almost daily.

• *Prolonged Stress:* Stress, in general, does not cause depression. In fact, people often are able to take on a number of stressful tasks and feel "okay." The key appears to be how you perceive yourself in the face of stressful situations. As long as you think, "This is tough, but I'm handling it. I'm making some headway," then stresses are seen as a challenge and you'll not likely get depressed. However, if you start to become overwhelmed or unable to cope with mounting pressures, your self-perception can change. It is probably the belief that "I can't handle this. I'm not in control. I'm totally overwhelmed" that triggers depression. When attempts to master stressful situations are inadequate, you may start to feel powerless, helpless, or out of control. Exposure to numerous or prolonged stressors, "plus" a self-perception of helplessness can set off a depressive reaction.

At times the reasons for depression are clear, but often they are obscure or hidden. It is clear that many human experiences can set the stage for or actually initiate depression. No wonder depression is such a common condition. You can take an important step in combating your depression by gaining some awareness of the causes. One of the most powerful ways to become more aware of the causes of your depression is to talk about yourself, your feelings, your past and recent events with another person. By exploring your own life and sharing this with another person, you may be better able to put the pieces together, to discover and to understand why you are depressed. Some people find that this can best be done in psychotherapy; others are able to gain this insight through honest conversations with close friends, family members, or clergy. The value in talking with another person about your life is two-fold. First, it helps to unravel the mystery and to make sense out of life experiences. Second, to quote a common saying, "Pain that is shared is easier to bear."

7

What Causes Depression?
— Biological Factors

D eep in the human brain are a number of important structures that play major roles in the regulation of emotions and various biological cycles. Two which are particularly related to our discussion of depression are the *hypothalamus* and the *limbic system.*

The hypothalamus is an incredibly complex brain structure about the size of a pea. It is the control center for numerous bodily systems (e.g., the hormonal system and the immune system) and physical activities (it controls or influences sleep cycles, appetite, sexual drives and the ability to experience pleasure).

Adjacent to the hypothalamus are the various structures of the limbic system. The limbic system is often referred to as the "emotional brain" because it is the seat of human emotions. When your hypothalamus and limbic system function correctly you are able to go to sleep and stay asleep, feel rested, have a normal appetite and normal sexual feelings, feel energetic and experience pleasure when nice things happen. Also, if you are faced with painful life events, you will feel sadness or upset, but not be overwhelmed (the limbic system helps to control emotions so they do not feel too intense).

The limbic system and hypothalamus are regulated by a delicate balance of various neurochemicals in the brain. Unfortunately several things can cause an imbalance or malfunction in these chemicals. When this occurs the result may be a biological depression. What can cause the system to malfunction? There are six major causes or triggers for such chemical malfunctions.

Medication Side Effects

Some prescription medications can inadvertently cause a change in the chemistry of the brain that triggers a severe biological depression. (Please see Figure 7-A for the names of medications that can, on occasion, cause depression.) Such side effects are relatively rare, but they do occasionally occur. If there is no logical reason for depression (i.e., no major life changes or losses) and the onset of depression followed the beginning of treatment with medications listed in Figure 7-A, then the medication is suspect. In such cases, the physician who prescribed the medication should be contacted.

Figure 7-A

Drugs that May Cause Depression

Type	Generic Name	Brand Name
Anti-Hypertensives (for high blood pressure or migraine) headaches)	Reserpine	Serpasil, Ser-Ap-Es, Sandril
	Propranolol hydrochloride	Inderal
	Methyldopa	Aldomet
	Guanethidine sulfate	Ismelin sulfate
	Clonidine hydrochloride	Catapress
	Hydralazine hydrochloride	Apresoline hydrochloride
Corticosteroids	Cortisone Acetate	Cortone
Hormones	Estrogen	Evex, Menrium, Femest
	Progesterone	Lipo-Lutin, Progestasert, Proluton
Antiparkinsons	Levodopa & carbidopa	Sinemet
	Levodopa	Dopar, Larodopa
	Amantadine hydrochloride	Symmetrel
Anti-anxiety Drugs	Diazepam	Valium
	Chlordiazepoxide and others	Librium
Birth Control Pills		Various brand names

Chronic Drug and/or Alcohol Abuse

A second common cause of biological depression is long term or heavy use of alcohol or other drugs. Certain so-called recreational drugs, for example cocaine and amphetamines, are well known for their ability to produce euphoria. However, with long term abuse, many drug users will experience serious depressive symptoms when they come down from a drug "high." Even more common is the effect of long-term or heavy alcohol abuse. Alcohol can produce very severe depressions; often such depressions lift after several weeks once alcohol use is stopped. (Note: If you have been using alcohol heavily and decide to stop, this should generally be done with medical assistance and guidance to avoid withdrawal symptoms).

Physical Illness

The third biological trigger for depression, physical illness, can contribute to depression in two ways (see Figure 7-B). They may cause brain-chemistry changes, and/or one may become depressed because of the effect of the illness. For example, a person with arthritis may have to endure daily physical pain. Serious heart problems cause people to dramatically alter their lifestyles. A person with a terminal illness will be facing increasing disability and death. Any such debilitating physical illness is likely to trigger psychological/emotional responses. However, in addition to these expected emotional reactions to illness, such disorders as those listed in Figure 7-B may actually cause chemical changes in the brain that set off a biological depression.

Thyroid disease is likely the most common medical cause for depression (possibly being a factor in up to 10 percent of people with major depression). Especially common and often missed is *sub-clinical hypothyroidism* which is diagnosed by a blood test which shows an elevation of TSH (thyroid stimulating hormone). Because of its high prevalence rate, it is a good idea for all people experiencing depression to have basic thyroid screening.

Primary Sleep Disturbances

Approximately 5 percent of the adult population suffers from *sleep apnea*. This is a condition in which the person's airway becomes obstructed during sleep, resulting in numerous episodes of interrupted breathing during the night (200-300+ episodes). Apnea is more common in people who are overweight or who suffer from high blood pressure, and almost always results in pronounced daytime fatigue and (in 45 percent of people with apnea) depression. This cause for depression is often overlooked and thus never treated. Also, when the primary cause for depression is sleep apnea, antidepressant medication treatment is often unsuccessful. The most pronounced warning signs of sleep apnea are snoring and daytime fatigue. Be sure to ask your significant other if you snore (many people who snore never know it). In addition to typical snoring, ask if you frequently stop breathing during the night (for 10+ seconds) followed by gasping. If sleep apnea is suspected, you should contact a sleep disorder specialist, since good treatments are available for this condition.

Additionally, be aware that sleep disturbances in general can be the cause of depression. The disturbances are commonly seen in pre-menopausal and menopausal women (especially those experiencing hot flashes), in new mothers (sleep deprivation is a major trigger for depression and for bipolar illness during the first two months after the birth of a baby), in people who work the night shift and have trouble sleeping during the day, and in individuals with sleep problems associated with drug use (sometimes, even minimal drug use); see Figure 7-C.

Hormonal Changes

You will note that listed in Figure 7-B are post-partum mood changes (following childbirth), pre-menstrual syndrome and menopause. These are not physical illnesses, but rather are conditions that involve significant hormonal changes. Depression is much more common in women than in men, and one reason *may* have to do with the influence of female hormones on mood. The incidence of depression among women has been shown to increase during major periods of hormonal flux (e.g., following the birth of a child). Some researchers suggest that up to fifty percent of women experience a minor but noticeable degree of mood change during the pre-menstrual time, and approximately five percent of women may undergo very serious depressive experiences during this time. Ten percent of all births are followed by the mother experiencing a severe post-partum depression. In ways that are not yet well understood, hormones often seem to affect the delicate chemical balance in the emotional brain, at least in a small percentage of genetically vulnerable women.

Figure 7-B

Diseases and Disorders that Can Cause Depression

Addison's disease
AIDS
Anemia
Asthma
Chronic Fatigue Syndrome
Chronic infection
  (mononucleosis, TB)
Chronic pain
Congestive heart failure
Cushing's disease
Diabetes
Hyperthyroidism
Hypothyroidism
Infectious Hepatitis

Influenza
Malignancies (cancer)
Malnutrition
Menopause
Multiple sclerosis
Parkinson's disease
Porphyria
Post-partum mood changes
Pre-menstrual syndrome
Rheumatoid arthritis
Syphilis
Systemic lupus erythematosis
Uremia
Ulcerative colitis

Figure 7-C

Drugs that Can Interfere with Sleep

• Alcohol*
• Bronchodilators (asthma medications)
• Caffeine
• Stimulants: Ritalin, Adderal, Dexedrine, methamphetamine
• Pseudoephedrine
•Tranquilizers*

* Note: Both alcohol and tranquilizers (see Figure 15-D) can help one to fall asleep, but they are notorious for decreasing the amount of time spent in deep sleep.

Stress Induced

Emotional stress, especially if it lasts for a long time, can also eventually lead to neuro-chemical changes in the brain. This is especially likely in two types of circumstances: (1) when a person experiences a major loss; (2) when faced with difficult challenges, the person feels powerless, helpless or overwhelmed. Situations that result in the experience of helplessness have been shown not only to produce strong biologic reactions in people, but in animals as well.

Endogenous Depression

Endogenous depressions (arising from within, in the absence of stressors) occur in certain susceptible individuals for unknown reasons. Such people periodically experience a tremendous neurochemical malfunction and resulting depression.

• *Recurrent Unipolar/Major Depression:* Some types of highly recurrent depressions may be due primarily to an underlying genetic/biologic cause. There is also increasing evidence to suggest that, with repeated, severe depressions, specific brain structures undergo marked changes (including the destruction of nerve cells in certain parts of the limbic system). These changes occur primarily in response to long-term exposure to certain stress hormones (such as cortisol) and brain chemicals (e.g., glutamate). Thus for some individuals, the initial one or two depressive episodes may have been clearly triggered by exposure to difficult life stresses. However over time, and in the wake of over-exposure to such hormones/neurochemicals, the brain changes. And such changes can result in increased biological vulnerability to subsequent depressive episodes that look "endogenous" (i.e., they erupt in the absence of significant life stresses).

Fortunately, medical treatments for depression can prevent depression-related brain damage and even promote the repair of brain tissue (see chapter 15).

• *Bipolar Disorder* is a particular type of endogenous biological depression formerly known as "Manic-Depressive Illness." Bipolar disorder is known to have a strong genetic loading (that's a psychologist's way of saying it tends to run in families). It is a type of depressive disorder that most professionals agree is almost entirely caused by biochemical malfunctions. Please see a more detailed discussion of bipolar illness in chapter 17.

• *Seasonal Affective Disorder* (S.A.D.) is a depressive condition hypothesized to be caused by changes in the amount of sunlight to which one is exposed. Do gray days get you down? Many people seem to have mild mood changes when it is cloudy outside; for others, gray skies and reduced sunlight can trigger very severe biological depressions. With S.A.D., depressions are often set in motion during the winter months when there is less sunlight available. It is also important to note that depression resulting from reduced light exposure occurs in many people who routinely work the night shift. Sunlight stimulates changes in the hypothalamus (a tiny but very important structure in the brain). These changes alter the neurochemical balance in the brains of certain individuals. For some, this decreased light sets in motion a severe biological depression. Some researchers are now prescribing "light therapy" for victims of S.A.D. This therapy consists of daily exposure to bright lights (intensity level required is 10,000 Lux). Patients sit three feet away from a bank of fluorescent lights for 20-60 minutes a day during winter months. The patients can engage in normal activities while exposed to this light. Such treatment has been shown to be helpful in patients who have true Seasonal Affective Disorder. An additional helpful approach is simply to go outside for an hour each day (even on cloudy days, outdoors there is ample light to help combat S.A.D.).

Please note that many people who suffer from seasonal affective disorder actually have a form of bipolar illness. Increased bright light exposure may relieve their depression, but may also provoke a manic episode (see chapter 17). Caution is advised in undertaking bright light therapy without supervision by a qualified mental health professional.

When biological factors such as those discussed in this chapter trigger depression, people can develop severe symptoms and yet often feel perplexed because they may see no logical reason to feel depressed. There are a number of good treatments — notably specific medications — which are available for biological depressions. These will be discussed in detail in chapter 15.

Figure 7-D

Summary: Causes of Depression

Predisposing Factors
  A. Early Life Experiences
      1. Early neglect
      2. Early losses
      3. Emotionally unavailable parents
      4. Pervasively harsh emotional atmosphere in the home
      5. Lack of support for growth
      6. Child abuse and molestation

  B. Heredity

Current or Recent Factors
  A. Interpersonal Losses
  B. Existential Losses
      1. Disillusionment/loss of a dream
      2. Awareness of one's mortality
  C. Events that lower self-esteem
  D. Physical Disease and Chronic Paine
  E. Prolonged Stress

Biological Factors
  A. Medication Side Effects
  B. Chronic Drug/Alcohol Abuse
  C. Physical Illness
  D. Primary Sleep Disturbances
  E. Hormonal Changes
  F. Stress-induced
  G. Endogenous Depression

Part Two:

What Can I Do To Beat Depression?

8

The Course of Depression and Relapse Prevention

While depression is a once-in-a-lifetime event for many people, in most depressions — about two-thirds actually — the depression may be constant or may return again and again (i.e., repeated episodes).

These persistent forms of depression are important to understand because they are so common, and because they lead to another major goal in for treatment. Goal number one, of course, is to reduce and eliminate *current depressive symptoms*. Those who experience persistent depression, however, have a second goal: to prevent *relapse*.

Thankfully, a lot can be done to break the cycle of long-term depression, but you need to know what you're dealing with to be prepared to take action. So, let's take a look at the various ways depression presents itself, and what that means for relapse prevention.

Snapshots on the Course of Depression

One way to get a picture of the course of depression is by way of timeline diagrams. Figure 8-A, for example, depicts a single episode of depression.

Figure 8-A

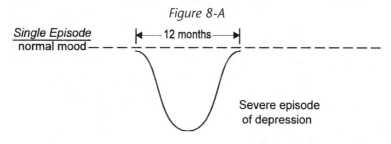

Untreated, most single episodes last about twelve months (treatment, of course, can shorten this time of suffering considerably).

Figure 8-B shows an even more typical pattern of recurring depressions. The time between depressive episodes may be two to-five years.

Figure 8-B

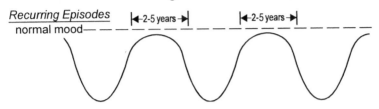

If you're having your first episode of depression, it's very hard to know if there will be other episodes later on, but there are some clues. Research has identified some risk factors that may predict a greater likelihood of subsequent episodes:

(1) a strong family history of depression,

(2) a first episode before age eighteen, and/or

(3) a very severe current depression with marked biological symptoms.

I do not mean to be pessimistic by addressing these issues, but it's important to know the facts. If you are in the "at risk" group, however, please know that there are very effective ways to avoid relapse, which we will address later in this chapter.

About fifteen to twenty percent of people who go through a *major depression* experience only partial recovery (even with treatment) and are then left with a chronic low-grade depression that can last for years (see Figure 8-C). In almost all cases, this condition can be remedied by aggressive treatment. Too many of these individuals unfortunately feel that they must just "endure" this less severe long-term depression. They need not. If this description applies to you, please take action. Newer approaches to medication treatment for depression have proven to be highly successful in taking these "partial responders" to full recovery.

Figure 8-C

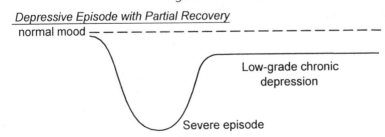

Dysthymia — a type of low-grade chronic depression that often begins in childhood or adolescence and can last a lifetime — is graphically illustrated in Figure 8-D. Sometimes dysthymia is labeled a "minor depression" — perhaps because it is a "low grade" condition and may not be acutely life-threatening. But that's a misnomer. This disorder affects three percent of the population and results in a *daily* experience of low self-esteem, low energy, lack of motivation, negative thinking and decreased sense of aliveness. Multiply these daily experience times the decades of one's life and we're not talking about a "minor" problem. Dysthymia robs people of aliveness and significantly affects those around them as well.

Figure 8-D

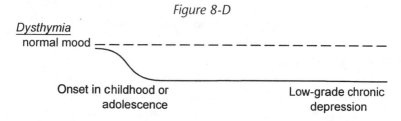

Folks with dysthymia can also periodically experience major acute depressive episodes. When the severe episodes pass, these patients return to their less-depressive baseline. This condition, referred to as Double Depression (see Figure 8-E) is also very responsive to treatment.

Fortunately there are treatments — including antidepressant medications — which have been found to be very effective in more than half of the people who suffer with this disorder. Those individuals in my practice who have had a successful response to medication almost always comment, "I have never felt this good in my entire life!" In such cases, this treatment is truly life-changing.

Figure 8-E

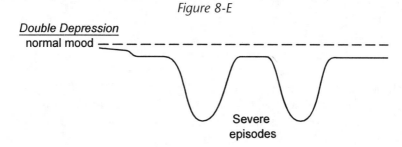

Finally, *Bipolar Disorder*, which was discussed in chapter 7, is illustrated in Figure 8-F, showing the severe mood swings between the depressive and manic states characteristic of this disorder (see chapter 17).

Figure 8-B

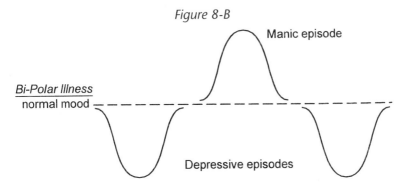

Manic episode

Bi-Polar Illness
normal mood

Depressive episodes

Preventing Relapse

Everyone I've known who has lived through an episode of major depression understandably is afraid even to think of going back through that kind of hell again. In all likelihood you won't have to if you know what you're up against and are prepared to take action.

The continuous or repeated episodic depressions described above are very common, so it is important to focus our attention on relapse prevention. There are three primary approaches I'd like to discuss with you.

Direct Action: It's very helpful to get clear about the particular life circumstances or events that have triggered depression for you in the past. Perhaps the most common situations that lead to depression are ongoing, troubled *relationships* in which you may be taken advantage of, ignored or mistreated. Another common set of events that may ignite depression is reduced involvement in *meaningful activities* (church, recreational pursuits, volunteer work, etc.) Healthy relationships and social involvements provide an ongoing source of meaningfulness in life. If allowed to deteriorate, these wellsprings of vitality may dry up bit-by-bit, gradually pushing you back into depression.

Think of it this way: If there is a fire in your home, you can just open the windows and let out some of the smoke — but it's a temporary solution. It's better to extinguish the fire directly. Taking action directly to alter life circumstances that may provoke depression is an important part of relapse prevention. Am I stating the obvious? Perhaps. But far too many people have a tremendous capacity to more-or-less ignore such problem situations until they reach a crisis level.

I'd like to encourage you to adopt this perspective instead: *"I owe it to myself to prevent recurrence of depression in my life. As one way to do this, I'm making a commitment to be on watch for any and all life circumstances that have the potential to hurt me emotionally, and then to do my best to directly address them. If the problems are not easily resolved, I'll consider seeing a therapist to help me formulate a plan of action. My emotional well-being is at stake here, and I'm not willing to ignore such issues if they come up in my life."*

If relationship problems are the source of distress, maybe the action to take is to actively pursue resolution of the issues that are dividing you. If the issues are serious and the relationship is very important (e.g., your marriage), resolution might best be accomplished through psychotherapy or marital counseling.

If the problem is a lack of social contacts or community involvement, the course is even more direct: get involved again. Seek out people in small groups with common interests: church, volunteer service organizations, music groups, hobby clubs, sports, theater, social groups . . .

Heed Early Warning Signs: A second key element in your campaign against relapse is to become very aware of your own unique "first signs" of recurrence — they vary a lot from person to person. Early warning signs often perceived by the person who experiences depression include: poor concentration, sleep disturbances, irritability, fatigue and loss of interest in usual life activities. Warning signs often noticed by significant others include: withdrawal, lack of affection/intimacy, irritability, moodiness, lack of follow-through with normal tasks (e.g., paying bills), and sleep problems. It is important to emphasize that the ability to catch a new episode early is crucial in relapse prevention, and it is often loved ones who notice the first signs. It will be important to speak with them about this and encourage open communication if any of these symptoms begin to reappear.

When such indications begin to emerge, your worst enemy is denial. *Don't ignore these warning signs,* because quick action is the antidote. At the first hint of recurrence, take steps to correct the situation. If *psychological treatment* helped before, contact your therapist and start again immediately; if *self-help approaches* were useful, pull out this book, refresh your mind and start working on them. If *antidepressant medications* were successful before, call your physician right away. Most recurring depressions can be nipped in the bud by taking decisive action before the depression gains strength.

Consider Antidepressant Medications: For people who have responded well to antidepressant medications, ongoing treatment with medications often makes sense to prevent relapse. The National Institute of Mental Health and the American Psychiatric Association practice guidelines now state that ongoing (lifelong) treatment with antidepressants is strongly suggested for all individuals who have had two or three episodes of major depression. Continuous treatment with medications has often been shown to be highly effective in preventing relapse in people with clear-cut recurrent depressions.

This may seem a drastic recommendation. However, if the depression is recurrent and major, the alternative may be to experience one episode after another — not the way any of us wants to go through life. Ongoing treatment has firm research support as a highly effective method of preventing relapse of major recurrent depression. (We'll take a more in-depth look at antidepressant medications in chapter 15.)

It may help to think of it this way: if you were diagnosed with diabetes, you know you'd be taking insulin the rest of your life. Isn't your lifelong mental health worth similar consideration?

In this chapter we've only scratched the surface of steps to consider in preventing relapse after a major depressive episode, or elevating yourself from a chronic lifelong depressive condition. All of the procedures outlined in this chapter and throughout Part II of this book are worthy of your consideration as you tackle the important task of preventing depression in your future. If you choose to say, "Been there, done that," and to put depression behind you, I urge you to consider these methods of prevention and treatment, find the ones that work for you, and follow them. You already know the rewards of keeping depression out of your life.

9

Choices About Treatment

Depression feels hopeless even though the prognosis is excellent.
— David Burns, M.D.

The majority of people who are depressed receive no treatment —
in fact, only one out of three depressed people get professional
help.

Some people may not recognize that depression is causing their
discomfort. For many people, depression is experienced only as a
physical illness. Some don't know that help is available, and many
cannot afford private treatment.

Normal occasional blue moods do not require treatment, of course,
such experiences being a natural part of the human condition. However,
more serious and prolonged periods of depression — as described in
chapter 1 — are reason for concern. Depression, in addition to causing
considerable emotional suffering, can also lead to serious problems in
functioning (sometimes jobs are lost and marriages ruined). Many good
parents find it difficult if not impossible to interact with and nurture
their children during times of serious depression. At times depression
can lead to a decreased resistance to disease and resulting poor physical
health. In some extreme instances the result is suicide. Thus it is very
important for you to be aware that *depression can be successfully treated in the
vast majority of cases.*

Many depressed people feel a tremendous amount of hopelessness
and believe, "I'll never get out of this depression . . . Nothing will help."
A feeling of hopelessness in itself is a *symptom* of depression and is not
uncommon. However, when you feel hopeless, keep in mind that this
feeling or *belief* is not a *fact.* Arthur, a recent psychotherapy patient of

mine, had experienced a tremendously painful depressive episode. After recovering, he said "When I was very depressed I was absolutely convinced that there was no hope for me. There was no way that you could have convinced me that I'd ever get over the depression. The hopelessness felt so real. Thank God I didn't kill myself, because I really am okay now." This is a very typical experience. Depression can result in a veil of darkness that clouds one's view of the future; but this sense of hopelessness is a *symptom* of depression, not a *fact*. What *is* a fact is that four out of five people with serious depression recover when they receive appropriate treatment!

Resources for Treatment

Although private psychiatric treatment or psychotherapy can often times be expensive, lower cost or free treatment is available in most cities in local public community mental health centers. If you would like help in locating a low cost treatment program in your community, here are a number of resources which may be of help. Look them up in your local telephone directory, or call directory information for a number:

Community Mental Health Center
County Health Department
County Department of Social Services
Hotline or Crisis Line Telephone Service
College or University Counseling Center
College or University Psychology Department Clinic
Family Services Center

Don't hesitate to call local psychologists, psychiatrists, clinical social workers, marriage and family therapists, clergy or others to ask their fees and/or to find out about low-cost services.

If you cannot find a local resource, please contact:

National Mental Health Association
1021 Prince Street
Alexandria, Virginia 22314
Phone: 1-800-969-NMHA

(Ask for the address of your local Mental Health Association)

Depression Awareness (D/ART) Program
National Institute of Mental Health
5600 Fishers Lane, Room 10-85
Rockville, MD 20857
Phone: 1-800-421-4211

Where To From Here?

Throughout this book I've emphasized that you have some choices. Depending upon the nature and seriousness of your condition, your options for treatment fall into two broad categories: *self-help approaches*, and *professional treatment.*

If after reading this far it is clear to you that you are depressed, what is your next step? Many mild forms of depression can be resolved within a few weeks by using the procedures outlined in the next few chapters. However, more persistent or severe forms of depression may be difficult to overcome without professional help. If you are √ experiencing any of the following signs or symptoms it will probably be best to consider professional treatment:

- A pervasive sense of dysphoria or despair, with absolutely no times when you are able to experience happiness
- Severe disruption in personal relationships or an inability to work
- Persistent and strong suicidal ideas
- Biological symptoms of depression such as significant sleep disturbances or weight loss (See chapters 1, 7, and 14)
- Profound hopelessness or apathy. Sometimes people may feel so hopeless or apathetic that it is difficult to start using self-help approaches.
- Symptoms of bipolar disorder (i.e., manic symptoms): see chapter 17.

If you're not sure which approach is best for you, why not schedule a single appointment with a professional and talk it over?

In the next few chapters, I will outline several self-help strategies that have been widely used in the treatment of depression. Depression is a bit like waging a war. It is important to attack the problem on many different fronts. The combined use of the various self-help approaches outlined in these chapters will give you a wide range of self-help strategies and ammunition for overcoming depression.

10

Healthy and Destructive Responses to Emotional Pain

It's inevitable that we'll all face both physical and emotional pains. Confronted with painful events, there are many choices about how to respond. Some choices can lead to healing, others may trigger a chain reaction of responses that lead to increased emotional pain — the type of pain that blocks growth and restoration.

Here's an analogy which shows the parallel between emotional and physical injury and healing. If you fall and skin your knee, one approach to dealing with the injury would be to avoid re-injury and infection at all costs by excessively bandaging the wound. This might provide some protection; however, several weeks later, if you were to remove the bandage, the wound would not have healed; it would still be moist and possibly worse than it was just following the accident. A wound needs the protection that a bandage provides, but it is also essential for it to be exposed to the air so that a healing scab can form.

Likewise there is a tendency for people to react to emotional trauma by *denying or suppressing their painful feelings*. A common example of this often follows the death of a loved one. One or several family members will not openly grieve — rather, they suppress their sad feelings. One reason is that they think, "Someone has to be strong and take care of the funeral arrangements. . . Someone needs to be strong to provide support and stability for the others." Unfortunately such people are often praised for their "strength"; "Oh, he's handling it so well. . . What a rock." Another reason for suppressing grief is that it is just so terribly painful that people may think they cannot stand the feelings. It's very human to dislike pain and want to avoid it.

What's so bad about denying or suppressing grief? Suppression of feelings is always a short-term solution; inner painful feelings do not disappear and, like the skinned knee, "over-bandaging" interferes with eventual healing. People who refuse to grieve almost always prolong the healing process. Such people will continue to have inner feelings of intense loss for a much longer period of time, are at high risk for developing physical illnesses, and often develop a more severe depressive reaction. Suppressing grief simply does not work.

Back to the physical injury for a moment. A second approach to dealing with the wound is to expose it to the air. However, as your knee begins to heal, you may re-injure the exposed wound by falling down again, or perhaps actually pick off the scab. Each time the scab comes off it is like a new wound that has to begin healing again. It is also possible that the injury will get worse, by becoming infected.

On an emotional level such re-injury or self-inflicted injury often occurs. While most people do not consciously or willingly re-injure themselves, doing so is extremely common. How does this happen? One way is to *re-expose yourself to the same painful situation*. An example is that of a woman married to an abusive husband. He is cruel to her, belittles her, ignores her, which is tremendously painful to her, yet she returns to him and experiences more of the same.

A second and very common way to re-inflict injury is the emergence of *excessively negative and self-critical thinking*. Mental health professionals have recently discovered a very common but unhealthy process which often begins in the early stages of depression. One's perception of the world and oneself becomes tremendously negative; all that is seen are personal shortcomings and inadequacies. The world seems black, the future bleak, and the person becomes extremely self-critical. A man whose wife has left him because he had an affair starts to berate himself: "I'm such a damned fool! What's wrong with me? I screwed up my marriage and I'm screwing up my whole life. I'm worthless — no damn good to myself or anybody else. I can't do anything right." He is hurting enough from losing his wife, but on top of the pain, he is punishing and belittling himself. A depressed person may not recognize such negative thinking, yet it can have a profound effect, significantly intensifying emotional pain. (This topic will be discussed in detail in the next chapter.)

Figure 10-A

Actions Which Block Emotional Healing

1. Denying or suppressing the painful feelings
2. Re-injuring yourself by
   a) re-exposing yourself to the same painful situation
   b) excessively negative and self-critical thinking

How can you help yourself *promote* emotional healing? People who live through difficult times successfully, even in the face of traumatic losses, find six key actions helpful:

• Fist, they *accept that it's normal to have painful feelings*. One of my patients, a woman whose husband had left her, stated this well: "It hurts like hell and I don't like the sadness, but it seems real normal to me to feel this way because I cared for him so much."

• Second, *they give themselves permission to feel those normal human emotions*. So many times people may think, "I should be over this by now," "I shouldn't let this get to me so much," or "What's wrong with me?" "I feel like a cry baby," "I should be strong," and so forth. In each instance the person does, in fact, experience an inner feeling, but tries to deny it, minimize it, or suppress it, perhaps by becoming very self-critical, e.g., "What's wrong with me . . . I feel so weak." The results are self-criticism and suppression of feelings.

• People who deal *well* with painful losses also allow themselves to *express the feelings*. Although the exact mechanism is not yet fully understood, psychologists do know that there is something healthy about expressing painful feelings, especially if you are able to share the feelings with a person who can listen, care, and not be judgmental. At times caring friends will respond by saying, "It'll be ok . . . Don't feel so upset. You'll get over it." The intentions are good, but the message is "You *shouldn't* cry, you *shouldn't* be sad." This denial of feelings is not helpful, and can interfere with the natural expression of feelings — and with healing.

• It is extremely valuable to *stay in contact with supportive friends and/or family members,* and to allow them to help. When you're trying to heal an emotional wound is not the time to be "brave" and try to go it alone!

• Another thing that aids in healing an emotional trauma is to *maintain a clear view of reality;* squarely facing the whole of one's life and one's self, both negative and positive aspects. A good way for many people to express emotions and achieve a clear and realistic perspective is to write in a journal. And the most helpful way to do this is to write in a manner that expresses your deepest emotions (a dry and factual account of events is not especially effective . . . rather, try to write from your heart.)

• A sixth key action which promotes healing is to *engage in problem-solving*. This may be difficult to do at times of acute grief or despair, but at some point it is very important. An example of this is the man who has just gone through a painful divorce. He is very sad about this break-up in his marriage and misses his wife, but has realistically faced the facts of his changed life and has let himself feel and express sadness. The problem solving begins to take place when he thinks to himself, "I feel so sad, but my life must go on and I want to think about what I can do to start putting my life back together. I know that I will have a lot of times when I am alone. I may need to learn to live with some of the pain of loneliness, but I also want to do things so that I do not have to be alone every evening." By planning activities with his friends, relatives, and his church, he is beginning to deal with the problem of being alone.

Figure 10-B

Actions Which Promote Emotional Healing

1. Accepting that it is normal to have painful feelings.

2. Giving yourself permission to feel your normal emotions, including pain.

3. Expressing your feelings to at least one other person.

4. Staying in contact with supportive friends and/or relatives.

5. Maintaining a realistic perception of your life and yourself. Journaling can often help.

6. Engaging in problem solving which promotes growth.

11

Can You Help Yourself?

In recent years psychiatrists and psychologists have developed a new approach to treating depression called "Cognitive Therapy."

This form of treatment has gained great popularity for two reasons: first, because *it works*. In a six-year study conducted by the National Institute of Mental Health, cognitive therapy was shown to be a highly effective form of treatment for mildly- to moderately-depressed patients. The effectiveness was equal to that seen in patients treated with anti-depressant medications (as reported in *Time*, May 26, 1986). A number of other independently conducted scientific studies have also shown this approach to be quite effective. (Dr. Aaron Beck's book, *Cognitive Therapy of Depression*, summarizes much of the research in the field.) Unlike some approaches, cognitive therapy has a solid base of documented effectiveness.

The second reason for the popularity of this approach is that, although it is a type of treatment offered by many professional therapists, *it can also be used as a powerful self-help approach.*

I would like to describe cognitive therapy to you and show you how to put this self-help approach into action for yourself. It has been my experience that most people can easily learn cognitive techniques because in many respects they are based on common sense. After reading this chapter you will be able to start using these techniques to decrease your depressive feelings.

A momentary increase in mood will not in itself cure serious depression. However, if you are feeling depressed and you are able to do something that in a couple of minutes leaves you feeling at least somewhat less depressed, this can increase your sense of power or control over your emotions, and spark hope. In addition, cognitive approaches applied over a period of several weeks can significantly reduce depressive symptoms. This has been documented in research.

I know that if you are feeling depressed, you may feel quite skeptical about any self-help approaches. Most people who have been depressed have tried a number of things to get out of their depressed mood, and have been frustrated when their efforts have failed. It's easy to develop a sense of pessimism and hopelessness when nothing seems to work. There are no approaches that will rapidly and totally alleviate a serious depression; however, many of the techniques of cognitive therapy have been shown to fairly quickly result in some elevation of mood. Please read on — and give these ideas a chance to work for you.

Negative Thinking Causes Depression and Makes It Worse
As you've seen in the first half of this book, some types of depression are caused by biological conditions or malfunctions. Ways to deal with those will be discussed in chapter 15. However, many depressions are triggered by environmental events. Sometimes these events are specific and easy to recognize, such as a divorce, being fired from a job or the death of a close friend or relative. Other "environmental triggers" may be less specific. For example, the gradual decrease in affection by a spouse over a period of years, or a slowly dawning awareness that your hopes and dreams may not come true (e.g., the hope that you will succeed in business or find happiness in a relationship). Most of the time, whether the events are specific and sudden, or vague and insidious, they represent losses or disappointments. Do losses and disappointments always result in depression? The answer is No! Most losses do lead to feelings of sadness, but there are important differences between feelings of sadness and true depression.

To begin understanding how your depression may have developed, let's consider a very basic fact:

"Moods are created by your 'cognitions' . . ."
— David Burns, M.D., 1980

The term *cognition* refers to a variety of mental processes, including thoughts, perceptions, beliefs and attitudes. Your perspective and the way you look at and interpret the events of your life will have a lot to do with how you feel. Let's consider an example: Two factory workers are exposed to the exact same event. Each man is notified that he will be laid off from work because the factory is being closed. Take a look "inside their heads" at the cognitions (thoughts and perceptions) of each man:

- Bob: *"Oh my God, this is going to be terrible. What am I going to do? I've got to feed my family. I won't be able to find another job . . . No one will want to hire me. I'm forty-five years old, and it's impossible to get a job unless you're younger."*

- Jim: *"This is probably going to be tough. What am I going to do? . . . Well, it may be hard to locate a job, but I have a good work record, and I have skills. I'm going to start planning now."*

Often when depression begins, a person reacts by beginning to think in ways that are negative and pessimistic. Bob has made several errors in his thinking that guarantee distress. First, he makes *predictions* that are quite negative: "This is going to be terrible;" "I won't be able to find another job," and "No one will want to hire me." Of course if these predictions were 100 percent accurate, he would have reason to feel very discouraged. But how does Bob *know* that these statements are *true*? Where is the evidence? Often in depression, negative pessimistic predictions are believed, and people react as if they are facts.

Secondly, Bob makes a *conclusion* about reality: "It's impossible to get a job unless you are younger." Is this absolutely true? Probably not, but at the moment Bob feels that it is, and the result is despair or panic. The reality may be that it is *difficult* to locate a job, but not totally *impossible*. Finally, Bob fails to consider the positive aspects. Of course he feels bad about losing his job — no one is likely to rejoice. While both men have something to feel upset about, Bob, by his excessive negative thinking has generated extra misery and pessimism for himself.

Jim responds very differently. He too acknowledges that loss of employment may be a tough situation to deal with; it never helps to deny problems or gloss over obvious pain or misfortune. However, he does not jump to overly pessimistic conclusions, does not make gloomy predictions, and is able to keep an awareness of some positive aspects. He maintains a realistic perspective. Although he is in exactly the same situation as Bob, Jim is able to take stock of his strengths, his skills, and his work record. He's ready to tackle his new job: *finding* a job. In this example I hope that it is clear how the way each man *interprets and thinks about* his situation can greatly affect how he feels.

Let's consider another example. You're flying across the country to visit your family. The plan is that they will meet you at the airport. Your plane arrives and as you get off the plane there is a crowded waiting area, but no one there to meet you. You wait thirty minutes and still no one has come to meet you. What may be going on in your mind? A lot of how you feel will depend on what you are thinking. Here are some possible thoughts and resulting emotions:

Figure 11-A

Left at the Airport

Thoughts	*Feelings*
1. "Oh my God, I wonder if they have been in a car accident."	1. Fear, worry
2. "Maybe I screwed up. Maybe I told them the wrong date."	2. Anger at yourself, guilt
3. "I can't believe it. They forgot!"	3. Anger at them
4. "Possibly they got stuck in traffic."	4. Mild annoyance
5. "I'm not sure why they are late, but I guess I'd better call them or take a taxi."	5. No strong feeling

---

In this situation you have no real way of knowing for sure what has happened. You'll try to figure it out, and may arrive at one of these conclusions. Obviously the particular feeling you have and the intensity of feeling depends not on the situation per se, but on the *thoughts you have* about the situation. As in possibility 5, some thinking does not involve predictions or conclusions, but rather may be aimed at problem solving.

"A Penny for Your Thoughts"

The most basic assumption underlying the cognitive approach to dealing with depression is that when you experience a stressful situation, such as a loss or disappointment, a chain reaction of cognitions is triggered. There are two possible courses that your mental activity can take. The first is that you perceive and think about the situation in a very *realistic* fashion. If your perception of reality is accurate, the resulting emotions will be normal and adaptive. The normal emotional response to a loss, for instance, is sadness or grief. Normal sadness, even though painful, can eventually lead to emotional healing. In normal sadness you will not be flooded with extreme pessimism, and will be able to maintain a sense of self-worth.

The second possible direction of your mental activity in such a situation is *distorted* in an especially negative and pessimistic way. Extremely negative cognitions, although frequently appearing to be valid, nearly always contain distortions. The *distortions* involve:

- unrealistically negative perceptions of yourself, of the current situation and of ongoing experiences,
- highly pessimistic views of the future,
- failure to consider positive aspects

Such negative perceptions, because they involve some distortion of reality, have frequently been referred to as "Cognitive Distortions." When people begin to make these errors or distortions in thinking and perceiving, the *results* are:

- extreme pessimism,
- erosion of feelings of self-esteem and self-worth,
- destructive emotions that lead to increasing misery and block healing

These are the experiences that usher in an insidious depressive process that typically leads to more and more emotional pain, rather than emotional recovery.

At the onset of depression there begins a chain reaction of negative cognitives — almost like a single spark that begins a bonfire — triggering an explosion of negative thoughts. When people are depressed, such negative thoughts occur literally hundreds of times a day, each time generating more misery and pessimism. And, like the bonfire, once it is started, the depressed person may actually throw on additional "logs" to keep it ablaze. The repeated, often almost continuous, negative thoughts keep depression alive and interfere with emotional healing. Like the continual removal of a scab mentioned in chapter 10, the wound is re-injured again and again.

The two paths of cognitive response to a painful event are summarized in Figure 11-B:

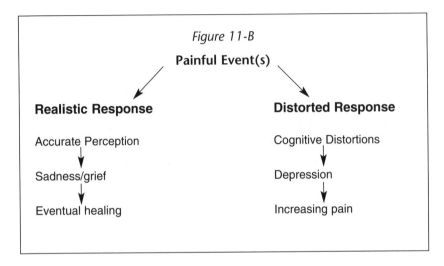

Figure 11-B

Painful Event(s)

Realistic Response   **Distorted Response**

Accurate Perception   Cognitive Distortions

Sadness/grief   Depression

Eventual healing   Increasing pain

Why would anyone intentionally do something that causes pain and blocks healing? The answer is that almost no one would if this were a conscious act. Most people are not aware that they are making cognitive distortions, however. Such thinking is not a conscious, willful act, but rather, such thoughts and perceptions pass through a person's mind in a very "automatic" fashion. This process is usually not in one's awareness and is thus beyond conscious control. It is also a process that can occur regardless of intellectual level; even people of superior intelligence can fall prey to such negative thinking. It has nothing to do with being "smart" or "stupid"!

The hopeful side, however, is that it is entirely possible to learn some systematic techniques that can effectively stop the destruction. Let's find out how.

12

Changing Your Negative Thinking

Simply being aware that negative thinking causes depression is not enough to stop the process. It will be important to take some specific steps that will allow you actively to combat the problem. The first step will be to become aware of those times when cognitive distortions are occurring. Let's begin by listing and describing the most common types of depression-causing cognitive distortions. (Much of this material is based on the work of Dr. Aaron Beck, 1979; and Dr. David Burns, 1980.)

Types of Cognitive Distortions
• **Negative Predictions:** This is the tendency to make highly negative, pessimistic predictions about the future, for which there is no evidence. Examples might include:

A single man asks a woman out for a date and is turned down. He thinks, "I'm never going to ever find anyone who wants to be with me."

A depressed woman thinks, "I've been depressed for months. I'm never going to get over this . . . nothing will ever get me out of this depression."

In both examples, the result is an increased sense of despair and hopelessness.

• *All-or-None Thinking*: This is the tendency to jump to broad, over-generalized conclusions about yourself or reality. Examples might include:

A woman has just turned in a report at work and her boss criticized the report. She concludes, "I can't do anything right." The reality is that she does many things right, in fact during the past week she has completed five other reports that were well done, but she focuses on the current criticism and arrives at the inaccurate and over-generalized conclusion, "I can't do anything right."

A recently divorced man spends a Friday night alone at home. He hoped a friend would call, but none did. He concludes, "No one gives a damn about me." The reality may be that he does in fact have friends and relatives who care a lot about him, but they simply did not call this night.

• *Jumping to Conclusions:* This is the tendency to conclude the worst in the absence of substantial evidence. An example:

A man applies for a job and is told, "We will call you on Monday if you got the job." By Monday noon he has not heard, and he concludes, "I know I didn't get the job."

• *Tunnel Vision:* This is the common tendency when one is depressed to focus selectively on negative details, to dwell on them and to tune out positive aspects of a situation or yourself. An example:

A middle aged man walks by a mirror and notices his pot belly. He thinks, "I'm disgusting. No wonder women aren't interested in me." The fact that he is somewhat overweight may be accurate, but at that moment in front of the mirror this is what he focuses on exclusively. He sees himself as disgusting. It very well may be that he is a kind and sensitive man, himself, not the whole person.

• *Personalizing*: This is the tendency to assume that if something is wrong, *you* are at fault; an assumption that may not be accurate. Example:

As a man comes to work, he says "hello" to his boss. The boss nods his head but says nothing. The man concludes, "Boy, he must be mad at me." This may or may not be an accurate conclusion. If he does not check it out with his boss, he may worry needlessly. It's a possibility that his boss is preoccupied or upset because of a fight he had with his wife. Many alternative explanations are possible. The point is that we cannot read each other's minds, and there is a strong tendency for people who feel depressed to overreact and personalize — especially when they fear criticism or rejection.

• **Should Statements:** This is the tendency to insist that things *should* be a certain way. Should statements may be directed toward yourself, toward others, or toward reality. Should statements can be recognized by the use of words such as: *should, shouldn't, must, have to* and *ought to*. Examples might include:

"I have to do an exceptional job at work, or I'll feel awful!"
"My wife ought to know how I feel — we've been married for twenty years!"
"He shouldn't have left me. I was so good to him. I gave my whole life to him!"

In each instance there is an insistence that things be a certain way. Should statements always have the effect of intensifying painful emotions; they never reduce misery or change situations.

Figure 12-A

Common Cognitive Distortions

1. Negative Predictions

2. All-or-None Thinking

3. Jumping to Conclusions

4. Tunnel Vision

5. Personalizing

6. Should Statements

Each of these cognitive distortions shares two things in common with the others: they distort in some way one's view of reality (resulting in a loss of perspective, and extremely negative and pessimistic views of oneself, current situations and the future), and each cognitive distortion has the effect of intensifying emotional pain. If unrecognized and unchallenged, such distortions in thinking will result in an ongoing destructive depressive process. It is very important to interrupt this process. The first step is to recognize such distortions as they occur. A major problem with cognitive distortions is that so often they are happening at an unconscious level. To break up the "automatic" quality of cognitive distortions, you first must become aware when they occur.

Even if you were to stop reading this book at this point, you would already know more about the types of cognitive distortions you probably make. That alone would help since you will likely catch yourself more often now when you make these errors. However, if you read on, you'll learn about some approaches that can help you break up this destructive process more effectively.

Becoming Aware of Your Cognitive Distortions
Many times people are not aware of the inner thinking that occurs during times of emotional pain. What *is* noticeable is the feeling. An important and effective method of becoming aware of cognitions involves using feelings as signals or cues. Here's a step you can put into action the next time you notice an unpleasant feeling. As soon as you notice such a feeling — for example, sadness or frustration — use this emotion to let you know, "OK, something is going on in my mind." Then ask yourself one or more of the following questions:

"What is going through my mind right now?"
"What am I thinking?"
"What am I telling myself?"
"What am I perceiving about the situation that triggered this feeling?"

Remember the example in chapter 11 about arriving at the airport? One person might start feeling very anxious and restless. She might say to herself, "I'm feeling pretty nervous. My friends aren't here to pick me up yet. What am I thinking? What's going through my mind? Well, I'm thinking that they are not coming and maybe they have been in a bad car accident."

This is a very important step. It's fairly simple, but often requires considerable practice. It is difficult if not impossible to change feelings directly, but you can very effectively alter your cognitions with practice. In order to do so, the first step is to make these inner thoughts and perceptions clear in your mind.

Remember, to become aware: sense a feeling, tune into thoughts, ask the questions and find the thought behind the feeling.

Challenging Your Distortion

The most effective way to directly alter maladaptive cognitions is to get a piece of paper and draw a line down the middle. After you ask yourself, "What is going through my mind?" jot down all thoughts, word for word, on the left hand side of the sheet. Dr. Burns, Dr. Aaron Beck, and other cognitive therapists have referred to these initial thoughts/perceptions as "automatic thoughts," because they flow through our minds so rapidly as to seem automatic.

The next step is to look at the thoughts, and ask these questions: "Does this sound like a cognitive distortion?" and, "Is this thought accurate and realistic?" In the airport example (chapter 11) the person writes down the thought, and then thinks "That sounds like I'm jumping to conclusions. It's a broad conclusion not based on the facts."

The next step is to challenge the thought. Your goal is to force yourself to evaluate situations or yourself in a realistic way, keeping in mind that the ultimate goal behind challenging cognitions is to reduce excessive or unnecessary emotional pain.

I want to emphasize that your goal is *not* to gloss over or sugar-coat your perceptions of reality. It is important to squarely face reality, even painful events.

In this situation, you might say to yourself, "That sounds like I am jumping to conclusions. What are the facts? I know they are late. I don't know why. There are many possible reasons that they are late. It's possible they were in an accident, but I don't know that for sure." Then write down a more realistic, rational response in the column on the right side of the page (Figure 12-B).

Figure 12-B

Automatic Thought	Realistic Response
"They are not coming . . . maybe they've been in a bad car accident . . ." (Jumping to conclusions).	"There is no way to know if there has been an accident . . . there are many reasons that they may be late."

Can you do this in your mind? Of course, but I want to strongly emphasize that writing it down is *much more* effective. It makes the process more concrete and conscious.

There is a general guideline to challenging distortions, which is to ask, "How *realistic* is my thinking?" Identify the real facts, compare your thoughts with reality, and phrase a new, more realistic thought.

Here are some more specific ways you can challenge cognitive distortions:

• ***Negative Predictions***: Remind yourself that you cannot tell the future, that negative predictions are rarely accurate and always result in increased depressive feelings. Also ask, "Where is the evidence? What makes me think that this *will* happen?"

• ***All-or-None Thinking***: Challenge directly the all-or-none statement, e.g., "I can't do anything right." "Is that absolutely true? I can't do *anything* right?" Then focus on the specific problem or mistake and acknowledge it.

• ***Jumping to Conclusions***: Ask, "Where is the evidence? How do I know this is absolutely true?"

• ***Tunnel Vision***: Remind yourself, "I need to look at the whole picture, not just certain details."

• ***Personalizing:*** Remind yourself that it is common to personalize when you feel depressed, but that many times others' reactions may not be due to you. "There may be other explanations and I certainly cannot read minds."

• ***Should Statements:*** The best way to challenge this is to acknowledge that many things happen that are very unpleasant, but this doesn't mean they should or shouldn't be. It's more adaptive and less painful to rephrase your statement in terms of what you do or do not want.

Figure 12-C offers a number of examples of common cognitive distortions, and the "automatic thoughts" which result. Note how these various distortions could be challenged, and the examples of more realistic responses.

Figure 12-C

Automatic Thoughts	Realistic Responses
1. "I'm never going to find anyone who wants to be with me." (Negative prediction)	1. "I can't see into the future. All I do know is that *this* woman did not want to go out with me, and I feel disappointed."
2. "I've been depressed for months. I'm never going to get out of This . . . Nothing will ever get me out of this depression. (Negative prediction)	2. "I don't know that for sure. I have no proof that I'll never get better."
3. "I can't do anything right." (All-or-none thinking)	3. "That's not true. There are many things I do well. The fact is my boss criticized *this* report."
4. "No one gives a damn about me!" (All-or-none thinking)	4. "Is that true? The fact is that I wanted to get a call from a friend and no one called tonight. But does that mean that *no one* cares? I know that I do have people in my life who care."
5. "I know I didn't get the job." (Jumping to conclusions)	5. "Wait a minute. How do I *know* that? I can't read minds. It does matter a lot to me whether or not I get this job, but let's not jump to conclusions."
6. "I'm disgusting. No wonder women aren't interested in me." (Tunnel vision, Jumping to conclusions)	6. "Maybe it's true that I have put on weight and maybe it's true that the extra pounds are not attractive, but there's a lot more to me than just a pot belly. I'm a nice caring guy. I'm a hard worker, and a good provider. It only hurts me to focus on my weaknesses. I need to remind to myself to look at all of me."
7. "He must be mad at me." (Personalizing and Jumping to conclusions)	7. "Maybe he's mad at me, but there might be other reasons why he acted that way."
8. "I *have to* do an exceptional job at work." (Should statement)	8. "I want to do a good job."
9. "My wife should know how I feel." (Should statement)	9. "I want her to understand, but she can't read my mind."
10. "He shouldn't have left me!" (Should statement)	10. "I didn't want him to leave and I feel sad and angry that he did."

"The Other Woman . . ."

Let's examine another example of how cognitive distortions are self-defeating. Take a look at two women who have experienced the same painful situation: after twenty-five years of marriage, their husbands have just left them for younger women. Let's be frank about this. Under any circumstances (regardless of how realistic your thinking is) this would be very painful. However, confronted with this loss, each woman has a choice about how to view her situation and herself.

KATHY:
Thoughts and Perceptions

Kathy often thinks . . . "I loved my husband very much." (Statement of feelings) "He shouldn't have left me. I gave my whole life to him." (Should Statement) "Obviously I just don't have what it takes to please a man." (All or none) "He probably has been turned off by me for years." (Jumping to conclusions). "I'm going to be alone for the rest of my life . . . No one will ever want to be with me." (Negative predictions) "He doesn't care about me." (Possibly accurate). I'm sure no one else does." (All or none)"I feel so terrible . . . I'll never get over this sadness." (Negative prediction).

BETTY:
Thoughts and Perceptions

Betty often thinks, "I loved my husband very much. I am very sad that he has left me." (A statement of feelings. No cognitive distortions) . . . "I am not sure why he left me . . . It may be a very hard adjustment . . . I'll probably be alone a lot . . . I'll need to think about how I can deal with the alone time." (Some realistic predictions and she begins to plan how she will cope). "I don't know what the future holds. I do know I am a good person, and have been able to make friends in the past. At some point in the future, I'm sure I will again . . . It's human to feel sad . . . it's ok to cry."

KATHY:
The Results

1. Intense sadness.

2. Erosion of feelings of self-worth and self-esteem. Kathy has convinced herself that she is so inadequate that she is unlikely to try reaching out to others. This may develop increasing withdrawal from other people.

BETTY:
The Results

1. A good deal of sadness and possibly anger toward her husband. Betty lets herself cry and grieve over her loss.

2. Betty maintains a sense of self-worth.

3. Pessimism and hopelessness about the future.

3. For Betty, the future is uncertain but is not bleak. A woman who was in therapy with me, one who fits Betty's description, once said, "I don't think anyone will ever fill the spot in my heart where my husband was for twenty-five years . . . but thank God I was able to realize that I do have others who care."

4. Kathy denies or minimizes other relationships that she may have in her life. Let's say that she does in fact have a number of good friends, several children, and a sister who cares about her. Does having these other people in her life erase the pain of the loss of her husband? Of course not, but at a time of sadness and loss, connections do help.

4. Betty maintains contact with friends and family, who support her in her pain.

Betty will surely have times where she feels a surge of sadness and loss. She will cry, and she will feel alone. But she also will heal. Kathy has suffered this painful loss too, but she continues to belittle herself, is flooded with pessimism, and has become more and more withdrawn. This is self-induced depression. She does not need nor deserve this additional pain.

Let's take a look at how Kathy might begin to fight back against the flood of cognitive distortions. She first must decide, "I am hurting enough because of my loss . . . I am not going to allow myself to suffer more than I have to." She can begin to challenge her negative thinking frequently. Whenever possible, as soon as she notices an unpleasant feeling, she can take a moment and write down both the automatic thoughts and a realistic response. If she cannot do it on the spot, she may do it later in the day, taking ten to fifteen minutes at the end of the day and going back over the events of the day and her thoughts. Figure 12-D summarizes the process.

Figure 12-D

Automatic Thoughts	**Realistic Responses**
1. "I loved my husband very much."	1. "This is accurate and true."
2. "He shouldn't have left me."	2. "It's not a matter of whether he should or shouldn't leave, the fact is that he did and I did not want him to."
3. "Obviously I just don't have what it takes to please a man."	3. "It's not obvious! For some reason he left me, but I don't really know why. Maybe he was not pleased with me, but if so he is just one man. Where is the proof that I don't have what it takes to interest other men?"
4. "He probably has been turned off to me for years."	4. "I don't know this to be a fact I can't read his mind."
5. "I'm going to be alone for the rest of my life"	5. "Where is the evidence? I can't predict the future. I'm not totally alone and I do not know what the future holds."
6. "He doesn't care about me."	6. "This is probably true."
7. "I'm sure no one else cares about me."	7. "Is this absolutely true? No. The fact is that a number of people do care about me."
8. "I feel so terrible . . . I'll never get over this sadness."	8. "I have no way of knowing how I'll feel in the future. It'll only hurt me to predict doom and gloom. All I know for sure is how I feel right now."

Going through the process of writing down and analyzing her negative reactions, in all likelihood, will help Kathy feel somewhat better within a few minutes. Often my patients have told me, "When I finished writing down the realistic responses, I did feel less upset. It didn't seem as if things were so hopeless or overwhelming. And it did feel good to do something to help myself feel better. But the fact is that I did still feel sad; not *as* sad, but sad."

The reality is that losses are painful. People care a lot about close relationships, and broken hearts do not mend quickly. The point, however, is that Kathy will be able to ease her pain and will notice some improvement in her mood almost immediately. But confronting her negative reactions just one time will not be enough. She may have to come back to these same cognitions each day for a few weeks, again and again hammering away at them, challenging and correcting distortions. Little by little this process can put a stop to the depression caused by these distorted ideas. For most people who decide to relentlessly challenge such distortions on a day-to-day basis, many depressive symptoms will subside in a matter of a few weeks.

Finding Balance in a Negative World

As mentioned earlier, one common aspect of distorted thinking that occurs for almost all depressed people is an inability to really notice positive aspects in daily life. Consider the following example: two men experience the exact same events; they have decided to take their son to a movie on a Saturday afternoon. On the way to the theatre, there is a traffic jam, and they begin to run late. At the movie theatre they have a hard time finding a parking space, which causes further delays. Eventually they get to the box office only to discover that all tickets have been sold and they cannot see the movie.

Who wouldn't be frustrated or disappointed? Let's see how this is perceived through the eyes of Bill and Matt.

- Matt's inner thoughts: *"I can't believe this is happening. The one time I try to do something nice for my son and first it's the traffic and now we can't see the show. It's ruined our whole day . . . I can't believe how angry I feel!"*

- Bill's inner thoughts: *"This is really disappointing! But don't let this completely ruin the whole day. The truth is that we missed the show, but I do have time with my boy . . . let me think . . . it's a beautiful day. Maybe we can go and play miniature golf instead."*

Bill was upset and disappointed; of course. But he was also able to step back from his emotions for a moment, gain perspective, acknowledge at least two good things (I'm here with my son and it's a beautiful day) and then engage in some active problem solving. This helped his mood and saved the day.

Depression often causes a marked loss of perspective. People get swallowed up in the emotions of the moment, only focus on the negative, and fall into a downhill spiral.

Again I must emphasize that the approach suggested is not some simple minded or unrealistic, "look on the bright side of life" strategy. It starts with honestly acknowledging the truth of the situation and one's emotional responses to it. But it then moves ahead with a focus on two questions:

- Given what's happening, what can I also acknowledge as positive?
- What other options can I consider that might make a difference?

Reality Is the Path to Healing
The best way out is through. — Robert Frost

Often, as I have worked with people suffering from depression, I have heard them say, "I don't know what is wrong with me . . . I shouldn't be feeling so bad." The person is suffering but also attempting to deny pain. Many times the turning point in therapy is to stop the denial and face the reality of the loss. One woman who lost her daughter in a car accident kept saying, "Crying doesn't help. She's gone. I need to be strong and get on with my life." One day it dawned on her what she was saying. She said to me, "Of course I'm sad! *I've lost my little girl.* How else is a mother supposed to feel?" She cried. This is not a cognitive distortion, this is honest grief.

There is nothing more human than to cry if you have lost a loved one; nothing more natural than to feel disappointment if you have failed at some important task, and nothing more understandable than to feel angry if someone hurts you or uses you. The open expression of feelings, when not clouded by cognitive distortions, is not only natural and human, but is also tremendously important. Honest grieving and feeling, even though sometimes very painful, promotes eventual emotional healing.

Choosing to battle depression by *challenging cognitive distortions* and, at the same time, *giving yourself permission to have and to express human f*eelings are choices that can lead to emotional recovery from depression. There *is* realistic hope.

13

More Self-Help Approaches

The several techniques described in this chapter, while not usually as powerful as the cognitive procedures described in chapter 12, can be helpful in your battle against depression on a day-to-day basis. You may find one or more will give you additional strength to help beat your depression.

Positive Activity Diary

Annie is a thirty-five-year-old woman who came to see me complaining of depression: "I can't get anything accomplished. I'm at home all day with the kids. By the time my husband gets home, the house is a wreck. I look at my house and think, what's wrong with me. I don't even work. I'm just a housewife and I can't get anything done. I feel out of control of my whole life!" Annie has three children, ages one, two and four. It was hard for me to believe her statements, "I don't even work, and I can't get anything done." She considered herself an inadequate mother and housekeeper, "who does nothing productive."

I asked Annie to start keeping an *activity diary,* at least for one day. I asked her to write down *everything* she did, even small things like picking up a toy or getting a drink for one of her children. She brought to our next meeting a small notebook with many pages filled. She said, "I can't believe it. As I was writing everything down, it hit me. I'm continuously busy from morning 'til night. Maybe my house looks like a wreck, but at least I know that I'm working my butt off. I *am* getting a lot done each day."

Many people, especially if they feel depressed, tend to overlook or minimize their accomplishments. Such a person may get to the end of the day and conclude, "The day was wasted, I got nothing done." This perception increases feelings of low self-esteem. An activity diary can help present a more realistic view of events.

There are two ways you can do this. First, to use the approach Annie used: write down every single activity. This does take some time and is not a practical thing for most of us to do on a regular basis. But doing it for a day or two can be helpful, as it was for Annie. A more practical approach for use on a daily basis is to record the major events of each day in a small notebook. In particular, record the following types of events: *tasks completed* (or progress made towards completion); *positive events,* such as receiving a compliment, having a nice lunch with a friend, getting a letter, feeling good about a job well done; and *mastery experiences,* such as, you were feeling sad, you took a couple of minutes, used the "two-column" technique (Figures 12-B, 12-C, 12-D) and felt somewhat better. You could write in the book: "Was able to get myself out of a blue mood."

This process works best if you keep it simple and easy. It is best to jot down only very brief three- to five-word statements. Then, review the list at the end of the day. Even very depressed people who feel as though they accomplished absolutely nothing in a day are often surprised to find out that in fact they have done many things or experienced some moments of pleasure. This approach is very easy to put into action and can give immediate pay-offs. It is an important way to counter certain cognitive distortions, especially Tunnel Vision or All-or-None Thinking.

Mood-Rating Chart
People who are depressed commonly look back over a period of time and remember primarily the negative feelings and events. They tend to conclude, "I've had an awful week. Everything went wrong. The whole week was terrible." This type of memory, which accentuates unpleasant experiences, can actually make depression worse. Believing that nothing positive happens in your life, or that you are always extremely depressed, can result in increased feelings of despair and pessimism. The fact is that *even very depressed people are not 100 percent depressed all of the time.* Even during a period of significant depression, people experience ups and downs. A person's mood is almost never completely stable. It is important and helpful to have an accurate and realistic

perception of one's moods and to be able to monitor changes in mood over a period of time. An effective way to accomplish this is the use of a *daily mood rating chart*. A number of studies have demonstrated that simply tracking and rating one's moods on a daily basis has the effect of decreasing depression. At first glance this might seem absurd, but let's look at this approach and understand how keeping track can help.

The use of a mood rating chart is simple. Take a look at the sample chart, Figure 13-A. (Feel free to make copies of this chart for your personal use.) Place a copy of the chart on your bedside table, and each night take a few moments to review the day. Ask yourself: "Overall, how did I feel today?" and then rate your feelings on a scale of from plus 7 (extremely happy day) to minus 7 (extremely unhappy day). Most people will notice that there is a good deal of change in mood from day-to-day.

How can this help? Let's look at an example on page 87.

Daniel is a forty-two-year-old college professor who has been experiencing painful and debilitating depressive symptoms during the past month. When I first saw him, he said, "Every single day, I feel paralyzed with depression. I have no energy, no motivation and no happiness." During the next week he completed a daily mood rating chart and brought it in to the next session (please Figure 13-B). In looking at his chart, he commented, "There were several days when I felt extremely depressed, but now looking back over the week, there were a couple of days that were not terrible, and most of the time I was not at rock bottom." This chart was helpful for him in two ways. First, it helped him remember more accurately and realistically how he was feeling. He soon realized that his depression, while certainly a painful experience, was not 100 percent pervasive. This acknowledgment helped to inspire hope, and left him feeling not quite so powerless. Secondly, he was able to use the chart over a period of two months to monitor his recovery from depression. After eight weeks of treatment, he said, "I've been noticing that gradually, over the past weeks, more and more of my days are good days. I still can get discouraged or have a crummy day, but there definitely is a positive trend. I am feeling better."

It is important to have some type of yardstick to measure change and recovery. The depression checklist (chapter 4) is extremely helpful, and can be used every week or two to track improvement. However, daily mood charting offers a more frequent — and easily read — means of observing changes in your emotional state. As Daniel experienced,

Figure 13-A

Daily Mood Rating Chart Starting Date: _____

Mood Rating:														Days:
-7	-6	-5	-4	-3	-2	-1	0	+1	+2	+3	+4	+5	+6	+7	1
															2
															3
															4
															5
															6
															7
															8
															9
															10
															11
															12
															13
															14
															15
															16
															17
															18
															19
															20
															21
															22
															23
															24
															25
															26
															27
															28

+7 Best day of my life

0 Neutral

-7 Absolutely worst day of my life

Figure 13-B

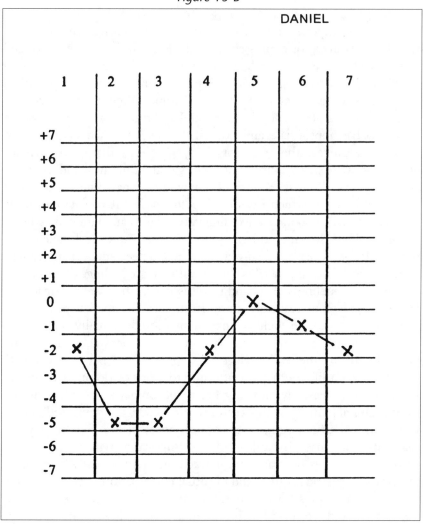

recovery from depression does not mean that at some point there are no bad days. Most non-depressed people have occasional days when they experience a low or blue mood. However, what one looks for in recovery is that gradually the good days come to outweigh the bad.

Staying Active and Avoiding the "Apathy Cycle"

When people experience grief or depression, a common reaction is to withdraw. Grieving or depressed individuals often limit their social and recreational activities, withdraw from meaningful involvement with others, and physically shut down. A part of this reaction is probably a natural desire to be alone with one's pain. Often it is difficult or embarrassing to be around others during times of distress. Some withdrawal is appropriate and normal, however marked or prolonged withdrawal can set the stage for many problems that tend to make depression worse. In a number of ways, social withdrawal and inactivity almost always do make depression worse. I have often observed a sequence of events which I call the "apathy cycle." If you start avoiding people, they will respond by avoiding you. Friends and family may begin to think, "He just wants to be left alone." The result can be increasing social isolation. Most people inwardly want and need support and contact with others. However, social isolation can increase feelings of alienation, sadness, and loneliness. A second result is that withdrawal and inactivity leaves the person increasingly cut off from positive experiences.

Some psychologists believe that depression is actually *caused* by a reduction in the amount of pleasant life experiences (Lewinsohn and Graf, 1973). In the early stages of depression, a person begins to withdraw from life, perhaps continuing to work or do other necessary tasks, but progressively allowing life to become void of pleasant and meaningful activities. As this continues to occur, the depressed person begins to feel an emerging sense of emptiness in life. Finally, physical inactivity can cause physical problems. Physical activity is required to stimulate the digestive tract, and marked inactivity actually contributes to decreased gastric motility and eventual constipation (a very common problem for depression). Where some inactivity and rest in non-depressed people results in increased energy and rejuvenation, it has the opposite effect in depression. Oversleeping and inactivity only operate to intensify the sense of fatigue. As one of my patients said, "It's like I'm having an energy crisis."

Often the apathy cycle is triggered by a belief or conclusion. There are three primary conclusions that can set this process in motion:

• **"People don't want to be around me."** Unfortunately, sometimes, this belief is true. It is often difficult for others to know what to say to a person who is going through a depression. But the conclusion may not be completely factual; it may be a cognitive distortion — and a self-fulfilling prophecy. If one believes that others do not want to be around him, it becomes an easy decision to stay at home and avoid contact.

• **"If I am around others I won't have anything to say. I'll be a bore."** Many depressed people feel that they do not have much to offer. A person whose ability to be witty or engage in lively conversation is affected by depression may predict that others will notice this and not enjoy her company.

• **"I feel too exhausted."** Most of the time, the inactivity and withdrawal seen in depression are the result of marked fatigue and low energy. One may know, intellectually, that to get out and about, to accomplish tasks or engage in an enjoyable activity will help improve his mood. But there is a critical moment in which he makes the decision to either take action or to withdraw. At such a moment, the perception of low energy and fatigue lead this person to think, "I'm just too tired." One of my patients, Dale, described this well. "On Saturday mornings, when I don't have to go to work, I'll get up. In the back of my mind I know I'd feel better if I could just do something like clean up my house or mow the lawn or go out to visit one of my friends. But I just feel so exhausted, so drained. No energy. I just fall on the couch and think, 'What the hell' and end up moping around the house all day. By Saturday night, I start thinking that I've wasted the whole day, and I feel even worse."

It is very important to get mobilized and to stay active. This, however, may be easier said than done. I cannot emphasize strongly enough how depression can rob one of a sense of motivation, enthusiasm, and life energy. Many times the profound fatigue is much more than a state of mind; it is a true physical symptom. So, how can someone who is depressed get moving?

The first important thing to keep in mind is not to wait "until you feel" motivated to do something. If you wait to feel motivated, says Dr. David Burns (1980), you may be waiting a long time. Most people find that if you can get started taking some action, your movement itself will result in increased energy. The problem, in a sense, is getting over the hump; i.e., getting beyond that initial feeling of inertia. There is a critical moment or decision point when you may think, "People don't want to be around me," "I won't be able to accomplish anything," "It won't be fun," or "I'm just too exhausted." Giving into believing these thoughts can stop you dead in your tracks.

What is very helpful at this critical moment is to say to yourself: "Just *do* it!" It may be helpful to write these words on an index or business card, and at moments of low motivation or apathy, get it out and read them. Keep in mind, "I don't have to feel motivated. Just get moving and it will feel easier." Even going out and walking around your house once or twice can energize you and give just enough of an energy boost to help you get started.

Building a Support System

A final helpful action that you can take is to enlist the help of a friend or relative. This should be someone that you trust. You might say: "I've been depressed lately and one way this has affected me is that I'm getting withdrawn. I'm not getting out and about. I know if I can push myself to get out doing things on the weekend, I will feel better. But, I need your help." A good plan is to decide upon some activity, for example going for a drive in the country or going to a movie. Tell the friend: "I know that once I actually get out of the house I'll feel better, so I want to check in with you Saturday morning around ten o'clock. You don't have to do anything or go anywhere with me. I'd just like to stop by for a minute and touch bases with you." When you have committed yourself to this plan, you will probably feel some degree of obligation to your friend or relative. This helps. A number of my patients have told me: "Knowing that my friend is waiting helps give me a push to get going. And once I'm dressed and in my car, getting out starts to feel easier."

The first few times you push yourself to do certain activities you may find it difficult — neither especially fun nor enjoyable. But keep in mind that staying active is a potent force that can reduce depressing feelings. Dale, the man I mentioned earlier, made it a point to do something productive or fun each Saturday and at least one weekday night per week. He found it easier if he made plans with a friend. A commitment made it harder to cop out." After a few weeks, he told me: "Now, at the end of the day, I look back over the day and think 'I really got something accomplished' or 'I took some action and it made a difference.' I feel better about myself. Instead of waiting around, hoping to feel better, I know that I've done something and I feel better. I feel

I'm getting control over my life again." The energy and momentum gained from participation in pleasurable activities is a powerful force to overcome depression.

When Should I Consult a Mental Health Professional?

The basic self-treatment approaches outlined above have been shown to be tremendously helpful for many people. However, there are times when these approaches are not enough. If you are experiencing any of the problems listed below, please consult a mental health therapist psychiatrist, psychologist, family counselor or clinical social worker) as soon as possible. You may need only a single visit and/or evaluation, but do not put it off.

• *A pervasive sense of despair or sadness* with absolutely no times when you are able to experience pleasure
• *Severe disruption in personal relationships*
• *Inability to work*
• *Persistent and strong suicidal ideas*, or if you have made a suicide plan
• *Biological symptoms* of depression such as significant sleep disturbance or weight loss. (See chapters 1 and 7)
• *Profound hopelessness or apathy*
• *Signs of bipolar disorder* (e.g., manic symptoms)

Some people may feel so hopeless or apathetic that it is difficult to start using self-help techniques and strategies. In our clinic many people begin in individual treatment. As they start to have some reduction in depression, they begin using the cognitive techniques described in chapters 11, 12 and 13. Some people also find it helpful to work with a therapist or a therapy group as they begin to use these approaches. Individual outpatient treatment for depression generally involves meeting with a therapist on a once-a-week basis. Even if you are in therapy, you will likely find that cognitive techniques give you tools and strategies to use between sessions and can promote more rapid recovery from depression.

If you are depressed, you need and deserve all the help you can get. Work with the self-help approaches described in this book, and find a professional to provide additional support if you need it. More on that in the next chapter . . .

14

Psychotherapy and Other Professional Treatments

"What kinds of professional help are available and how do I decide?"

Basically there are two types of therapy that have shown to be helpful in treating depression: psychiatric medication treatment, and specific forms of psychotherapy.

• *Medication.* When depression results in certain biological symptoms, this is a sign that a part of the problem involves a bio-chemical malfunction. You may recall from chapter 2 that certain physical symptoms are particularly important: sleep disturbances; appetite disturbances; loss of sex drive; fatigue and decreased energy; inability to experience pleasure (anhedonia); and severe agitation or panic attacks.

There have been important advances in recent years in the understanding of the biology of depression, and psychiatrists and family physicians are now better equipped to treat depression with a number of new antidepressant medications. If you are experiencing one or more of the biological symptoms of depression noted above (and discussed in chapters 2 and 7), it would be advisable to consult a psychiatrist or a clinic where psychiatric medication treatment is available. (A psychiatrist is a medical doctor with training in treatment of emotional disorders, including psychopharmacology — medication treatment.) Another option is to consult your family physician. Many family doctors are trained to treat depression with antidepressant medications.

(Some are not. Be sure your doctor takes time to do a thorough evaluation.) Please also see chapters 15 and 17 for a complete discussion of medication treatment for biological depression.

• **Psychotherapy** (sometimes referred to as "Talk Therapy") can often be extremely helpful in the treatment of depression. Generally such treatment is offered by psychiatrists, psychologists, social workers and licensed counselors. (Some clergy are trained in pastoral counseling and may be of help.) How can psychotherapy help? First and foremost, in psychotherapy there is a close and supportive relationship between the patient and the therapist. So many times, depressed persons feel extremely alone and alienated. The sense of support, connection and caring in a one-to-one relationship can help sustain you through very difficult times. Support is only one aspect of treatment that can be helpful, however.

During psychotherapy people are able to learn more about themselves, and to discover patterns in their lives that might frequently re-expose them to depression. Brenda is a twenty-six-year-old single woman who reports recurring feelings of depression. Most of these feelings have been triggered by repeated disappointments in relationships. She inwardly feels a great need to be loved and cared for by a man. However, in the past three relationships she has chosen to become involved with men who have chronic unemployment and alcohol abuse problems. Each time she has entered the relationship optimistically, only to find that after several months she ends up financially supporting him and getting few if any of her needs met. In two instances the men have been physically abusive to her, and each relationship has ended with a sense of loss and disappointment. In her psychotherapy sessions, Brenda has come to understand that one of her strong and important inner needs is to feel loved, and that in each relationship it had been her hope that by "rescuing" this down-and-out man, she would be rewarded with his love and gratitude. She now understands that her choices of men were doomed from the start because each man was extremely selfish and basically incapable of expressing true give-and-take in a relationship. Knowing this has been important for Brenda because it may help her make better choices about relationships in the future and act as a potent factor in preventing future depressions.

Many times people experience painful life events, but deal with the hurt by burying the feelings. Karen's husband died suddenly eighteen months ago. She thought she handled this loss well: "Of course I was sad, but I more-or-less got over it in a few months." She entered therapy with a severe depression and did not know why. During the first few weeks of psychotherapy, as this thirty-two-year-old woman talked about her life, she became increasingly aware of tremendous inner pain. Consciously she had thought she was over the death of her husband, but blocked grief often turns into depression. The most important things that happened in therapy for Karen were to become aware of her continuing inner grief and to allow herself to open up and mourn. After eight weeks of therapy she said to me "I know now that I'd locked a lot of sadness inside of me and I feel it more now. But I'm not depressed." Her more severe depressive symptoms lifted. Understanding hidden causes for depressive feelings is an important outcome in psychotherapy.

Life often confronts people with difficult circumstances: troubled relationships, work stresses, serious medical problems, — any number of significantly stressful situations. As we've talked about earlier, while stress alone generally does not lead to feelings of depression, if one begins to feel a sense of powerlessness or helplessness, depression can often be triggered.

Many people have voiced this situation to me this way, "It seems that no matter what I try, it just doesn't seem to help. I start to get on top only to feel knocked over again." One of the most important issues addressed in psychotherapy is this state of perceived *helplessness*.

For many people, simply being able to *speak out* about the pain and struggle, and to feel heard and understood, is helpful. There can be something empowering about saying, "This is happening to me, it hurts and I hate it." Beyond this, in many if not most psychotherapies, the patient and therapist together focus on *action plans* — developing strategies for taking direct action in one's life to resolve ongoing problems.

Taking action can be a hard step on your own, especially if you're feeling engulfed in depression. But many people find that action plans in their lives — perhaps with the help of a therapist — puts them back in control and helps give them a sense of confidence to manage their lives once again.

On another level, lots of folks live lives that are not in keeping with their own inner needs and values. Many of us drift into jobs, lifestyles or relationships that aren't really in synch with our true desires or ambitions. This situation may go more-or-less unnoticed for years, contributing to a growing sense of *dis-ease,* in which life feels progressively less meaningful and less vital. An important aspect of therapy for such an individual is becoming able to discover the truth of his or her *inner self.* Such self-discovery — coming to know in your heart of hearts what you really want, desire and need to feel alive — can be the most valuable result of a course of psychotherapy.

Loraine worked for years as a bookkeeper and often knew that she wasn't especially happy with her work; even though it was "okay" overall. At age forty-three, however, she became increasingly depressed and sought psychotherapy. As she progressed in therapy, she began to listen to her own inner voice. Her therapist encouraged her to explore how she really felt about her life and it gradually became clear to her that her vocation felt meaningless and boring. Toward the end of six months of therapy, she got in touch with a desire she had held privately for many years: to work with plants as a gardener.

A year after leaving therapy, Loraine called her therapist to say she had followed her own heart. She had embarked on a new career as a landscaper. Courses at a community college and part-time work at a nursery led to the development of her own landscape maintenance business. She said, "I know now that my depression was really a signal to me that I wasn't living my life in the right way. It's been difficult and kind of scary to change careers, and I'm not making lots of money yet, but for the first time in years, I feel alive."

In each of the instances mentioned above, we cannot claim that depression was "cured," in the ordinary sense of the word. Rather, psychotherapy helped these people to understand the legitimacy of their despair, and to develop ways to confront their pain head-on, including the courage to grieve losses, to face inner truths, or to make lifestyle changes.

Each client ultimately did the work and the growing on her own, but they also had the help of a therapist who served as a guide through the often-difficult territory.

A final important benefit from psychotherapy is that, when you're feeling utterly hopeless and discouraged, a therapist can transmit a sense of realistic hopefulness. The therapist can help you evaluate choices and options in a realistic way. Whereas well-intentioned friends or relatives may give you the message that "You shouldn't feel so bad," or that somehow you ought to be able to snap out of it, psychotherapists understand about depression and realize that you can't simply "snap out of it." With this understanding they can help you realistically face and deal with your feelings in a non-critical and non-judging way.

Four specific types of therapy for depression have been developed and have a solid track record of effectiveness. Let's take a look.

• **Behavior Therapy** includes a number of procedures which can help to combat depression, particularly when the depression can be traced to specific life circumstances. Behavior therapists often employ procedures from psychotherapy or cognitive therapy, but their specific expertise emphasizes such techniques as activity therapy, assertiveness training, systematic desensitization, behavior monitoring, and various systems to reward steps taken to reduce depressed feelings.

The behaviorist's goals and methods are designed to get you "moving again." Since a major symptom of your depression is likely to be inhibited activity — staying home, avoiding other people, not taking part in normal social contacts, not accomplishing daily chores, not doing anything "just for fun" — activity therapy may be prescribed. Simple activities — such as grocery shopping or walking around the block — might be the starting point, with the plan gradually calling for increased involvement with others — such as going to church, to a lecture, or to another low-demand public event. Such activities don't require much active participation, but can help you see that you can derive some small measure of enjoyment from life. And that awareness offers a foundation for greater and greater achievements and more demanding activities, gradually rebuilding your capacity to have fun and feel happy again. (This behavior therapy technique is actually a supervised and systematic application of the "staying active" self-help approach discussed in chapter 13.)

Assertiveness training is a behavioral procedure which will improve your ability to get along with other people, and to get more of what you want from life. Francine had been depressed off-and-on for nearly two years, primarily because she had allowed herself to be used as a "sexual doormat" by every guy who asked — or forced himself on her. She just did not seem to be able to say *no*. When she finally sought help from a behavioral psychologist, they agreed that she needed to set limits, to stop letting others take advantage of her, and to begin to regain her self-respect. At thirty-six, Francine was not too old to learn some "new tricks." The therapist taught her assertive skills for dealing with everyday situations — returning defective merchandise, asking for favors, standing up for herself — and helped her apply the same skills to even more difficult situations — dealing with an unfair supervisor at work, saying no to an invitation for a date. Over several weeks of therapy, Francine began to recognize that she does have rights, that she can be in charge of her life (within limits), and that she's really not such a worthless person after all!

Other tools among the dozens in the behavior therapist's "kit" include systematic desensitization — a technique for reducing anxiety by gradual exposures to feared situations — and behavior monitoring — a logging of daily activities similar to the "mood rating chart" described in chapter 13. Behavior therapists believe that the most effective way to deal with most emotional difficulties is to meet them head on, treating each complaint directly rather than looking for "underlying causes." Behavioral techniques have proved effective for a wide range of disorders, including depression, and may be appropriate for your situation.

• *Interpersonal Therapy* is an approach that acknowledges the fact that often depression arises when people have chronically troubled or unhappy relationships. This form of psychotherapy, which has also been shown to be highly effective in the treatment of depression, always involves both members of a couple or an entire family. The focus is on helping people develop more effective styles of communication and better strategies for problem solving. When relationships become more successful, when problems are resolved or there is an increase in intimacy, depression often lifts.

• *Cognitive Behavior-Analysis* Therapy is a new and very promising form of treatment that combines elements of cognitive, interpersonal, and behavioral psychotherapies. Preliminary research shows it to be highly effective in treating depression.

• *Cognitive Therapy* can be provided by a psychotherapist individually or in a group therapy format, or employed as a self-help approach. Cognitive therapy as a self-help approach was described in detail in chapters 11 and 12.

Do You Need *Therapy? Do You* Want *It?*

Now that you know a little more about what to expect from various professional treatments for depression, you may be asking, "But do I *need* that kind of help.

For an answer based on your own evaluation of your situation, I suggest you refer back to chapter 4 and the "Depression Checklist." If your total scores for either Biological Functioning or Emotional/Psychological Symptoms place you in the "severe" category, I urged you to contact a professional as soon as possible. If your scores indicate "moderate" levels of depression, please seriously consider the possibility. "Mild" scores are of less urgency, but the fact that you are concerned enough to have read this book says something about your situation. Don't let your sense of helplessness or hopelessness keep you from a step which could help turn your life around!

If you think psychotherapy might help you, it's a good idea to make an appointment with a therapist for an initial visit.

Selecting a Therapist

Selecting the right therapist is very important, and there are four main steps to take in your search:

• Speak with your family doctor, pastor, friends, or others who may have contact with the professional community, and collect the names of two or three therapists in your area. In most towns, there will be a handful of therapists who have established reputations. It will be important to go to someone who is well recommended.

• Find out if the therapist treats depression, and what the person's credentials are (see "Types of Mental Health Therapists" below). Although most therapists work with people suffering from depression, not all are specialized in this type of treatment. For instance, some therapists primarily help people with marital problems or the treatment of alcohol abuse. In speaking with a therapist, it is perfectly okay to ask specifically about experience in treating depression. This is even more of an issue if you think that medication treatment may be indicated; psychotherapists who do not practice in medical settings may not prescribe medication and some do not fully understand or believe in medical treatment of depression. Many non-medical psychotherapists, however, are affiliated with hospitals or clinics where medication treatment is available, or have a working relationship with a physician and can make a referral if such treatment is warranted. If you have been experiencing biological symptoms of depression and are open to considering treatment with antidepressants, it will be helpful to ask potential therapists about their experience with and their feelings about medical treatment of depression.

I want to emphasize that, unfortunately, there are *some* therapists who are avidly opposed to medical treatment of depression, despite recent, convincing research that in many cases such treatment is highly effective. Certainly in many types of depression, medical treatment is not warranted, and concern for unnecessary drug use is not out of place. Nevertheless, it would be extremely unfortunate if you are experiencing biological depression and did not have access to appropriate medical treatment. The result would likely be a prolonged time of suffering.

• Once you have established that a therapist does treat depression, and satisfied yourself as to the therapist's credentials, the third step is to make a phone call and talk about your main reason for seeking out therapy now. Obviously, it is impossible fully to explain one's life circumstances in a minute or two, but the main reason for doing this on the phone is so you can see how the therapist responds to you. This first contact with the therapist is important; it may be possible to get some first impressions. Often times people feel anxious about making an appointment. Most therapists understand this and use this first contact to help put you at ease and tell you something about their practice (for example, how often they meet with people, their fees, their specialties, etc.). One of my main goals in talking to potential patients in advance of the first visit is to help them feel more relaxed about this decision to come see me, and to express my intent to work together with them.

If you feel reluctant to make an appointment, it is fine to simply call a therapist and talk for a few minutes and possibly share your apprehensions about coming in. If you still feel hesitant, keep in mind that when you go in to see a therapist, in a sense you are hiring him or her to assist you in a professional way. If for any reason you are not comfortable with the person, you don't have to go back. You are in control of that decision at all times.

• The fourth step in your selection process is your own evaluation of the therapist and the therapy process in general after the initial session. After talking to the therapist during the initial session, you will very likely be able to judge for yourself if this seems to be a good approach for you. The important things to look for during the first session are: "Does the therapist seem to understand me?" and "Do I have a sense of hopefulness about this kind of treatment?" No type of treatment can resolve depression immediately and it will take some time and effort on your part; but if your answers to the two questions are "yes," then there is reason to believe that working with this particular therapist may be beneficial.

Types of Mental Health Therapists

• *Psychiatrist (M.D.):* Psychiatrists are medical doctors who have received specialized training in the treatment of emotional problems, including both medication and psychological treatments. (It is possible for a physician to practice psychiatry without specialized training, however very few do so. Again, it is appropriate to ask about any professional's background of training and experience in dealing with your condition.) Most psychiatrists treat depression and other emotional disorders with medications. Some psychiatrists also can provide psychotherapy, behavior therapy, or cognitive therapy. "Board certification" is an advanced designation granted by the profession to those psychiatrists who are especially well prepared.

• *Non-Medical Psychotherapists:* These professionals treat emotional problems using various non-medical, psychological approaches (such as psychotherapy, cognitive therapy, behavior therapy). Many non-medical psychotherapists are well versed in psychiatric diagnosis and can make referrals for medication treatment. They do not *prescribe* medication, however (there are rare exceptions to this in some states). Among the non-medical specialists:

- *Psychologists:* Hold a doctorate degree in psychology (Ph.D., Psy.D., Ed.D.), have three or four years postgraduate training in psychological methods, and in most states are licensed to practice. They also have specialized training in the administration and interpretation of psychological tests. The most advanced designation for a psychologist is that of "Diplomate" of the American Board of Examiners in Professional Psychology

- *Clinical Social Workers:* Generally hold a masters degree (M.S.W.), have considerable supervised experience, and are usually licensed by the state (hence the designation, "L.C.S.W." — Licensed Clinical Social Worker)

- *Marriage, Family and Child Counselors/Therapists:* Some states grant a license to Marriage, Family and Child Counselors (or Marriage, Family and Child Therapists). Such therapists generally have at least a masters degree in counseling (M.A. or M.S.), usually with specialization in treatment of marriage and family problems or problems of children and adolescents.

- *Mental Health Counselors:* Some states also provide licensing for Mental Health Counselors. These therapists generally hold a masters or doctors degree in psychology or counseling.

- **Pastoral Counselors:** Some clergy have received training in counseling and may provide supportive therapy to members of their church or to others desiring a therapist who addresses both emotional and spiritual concerns.

A Final Note

Mike came to see me a month ago. He was severely depressed and had been for over a year following a painful divorce. He told me, "I started to call a therapist six months ago. I knew I was in hot water, but as I picked up the phone, I got cold feet. I was afraid to call and I said to myself, 'Oh, I'll be okay . . . I'll get over this on my own,' and I hung up the phone. This happened four or five times. I was just too scared and too ashamed to call. I wish I'd called you six months ago. My life has been like hell and I know I need help." It is *very* common and *very* human to feel apprehensive about making that first call.

Many people think, "Oh, I'm not that bad off" or "They'll think I'm over-reacting or feeling sorry for myself."

No one wants to feel foolish or embarrassed. But therapists know that depression hurts and that it can destroy lives. It's their business to take you and your depression seriously. Depression has a bad habit of dragging on for a long time, and not getting treatment when you need it prolongs the pain. If you know you are really depressed, make the call! Many times after a three-minute phone call, people can feel a sense of relief knowing that they have made that first step. Action is one of the best antidotes to feelings of powerlessness or hopelessness. Dialing the phone is a simple action you can take to help yourself.

15

Medication for Depression

A ntidepressant medications have well-documented effectiveness in the treatment of biological depressions and mixed-type depressions with some biological symptoms. The vast majority of people with biological depressions can benefit from the use of antidepressant medications. However, there is a good deal of misinformation and misunderstanding about the use of these medications. I would like to explain to you how these medications work to treat depression and to talk in some detail about such treatment.

Antidepressant medications represent a specific and unique class of medications. They are *not* tranquilizers, although they are unfortunately often assumed to be in the same category as Valium, Xanax or Ativan (which are minor tranquilizers). Antidepressants are chemically quite different and have very different actions than tranquilizers. Unlike some tranquilizers, antidepressants are not addictive or habit forming. Antidepressants are not "uppers" or "happy pills." Instead, antidepressants ease the intensity of some emotional pain, and eliminate many biological depressive symptoms such as sleep disturbances. While antidepressants can reduce anhedonia and restore the ability to experience pleasure, they absolutely do not produce feelings of happiness.

Many people are reluctant to take medications, stating: "I don't want to rely on a chemical crutch." Alcohol and some types of tranquilizers provide temporary relaxation or euphoria. In a sense these substances are "crutches" because, when the effects wear off, there is no lasting change — you're back to square one. However, this is not the case with antidepressants. In a real sense, antidepressant medications can produce lasting changes by returning certain parts of the nervous system to a state of natural and normal functioning.

Depression and Your Brain

Deep in the center of the human brain are a number of specific structures, such as the hypothalamus and limbic system, which make up the "emotional brain." These brain structures play important roles in regulating a number of physical and emotional functions, including appetite, sleep cycles, and sexual drive. They include pleasure centers and pain centers, operating to control feelings and emotional expression. When your emotional brain is functioning normally, you're able to get a good night's sleep, feel rested, have normal sexual interest and appetite, and not feel overwhelmed by intense feelings. In other words, you feel "normal." However, in biological depressions, such brain areas begin to malfunction and can produce a number of significant symptoms.

When confronted with the emotional pain of a divorce, death of a loved one, loss of a job, or other difficult situation, the picture can become greatly complicated if you start to experience the additional symptoms of biological depression. The task of coping with emotional pain can feel even more difficult and frustrating if you don't sleep, feel exhausted, and/or lose the ability to experience any pleasure.

How does this biological malfunction occur? The various structures making up the "emotional brain" must become activated or "turned on" in order to function normally. To use a simple analogy, let's say that you want to turn on a TV set, but the nearest electrical outlet is twelve feet away, so you use two six-foot extension cords. When these are connected end to end and then to the TV set, it can be turned on. The various structures of the emotional brain must be energized in order to appropriately regulate biologic functions and mood. This is accomplished by a series of nerve cells that are connected end-to-end, somewhat like the extension cords.

Electro-chemical impulses travel along each nerve cell until they reach the end of the nerve. The two nerve cells are not connected together like extension cords, however. The cells are separated by a tiny space call a "synapse." In order for the nerve impulse to be passed from one cell to the next, a type of stimulation must cross through the synapse. This is done chemically. Little containers called "vesicles" are activated by the nerve impulse in cell "A" and migrate to the edge of the

The beneficial effects of antidepressant medications are achieved primarily by restoring malfunctioning nerve cells to their normal state.

cell, spilling out a specialized neurochemical into the synapse (See "Activation of the Nerve Cell," Section 4 of Figure 15-A). The neurotransmitting molecules that have been implicated in some forms of depression include: serotonin, norepinephrine and dopamine. These chemical messengers drift across the synapse and attach to the surface of cell "B." When enough of the neurochemical attaches to cell

Figure 15-A

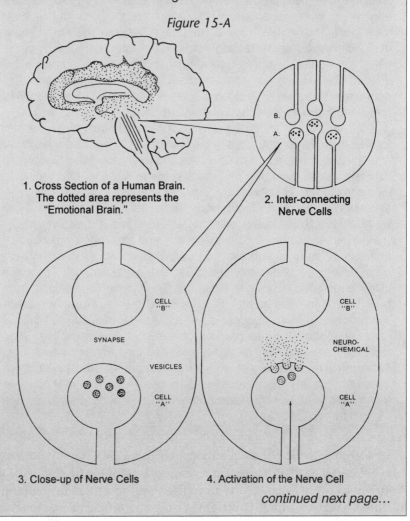

1. Cross Section of a Human Brain. The dotted area represents the "Emotional Brain."

2. Inter-connecting Nerve Cells

3. Close-up of Nerve Cells

4. Activation of the Nerve Cell

continued next page...

"B," it activates receptors on the nerve cell and has various effects. Such normal nerve stimulation must occur in order to maintain adequate, adaptive brain functioning.

Two problems occur in biological depressions. The first is something called "excessive re-uptake." For reasons that are not well understood, the cell begins to malfunction. Just after the neurochemical is released into a synapse, it is rapidly re-absorbed into cell "A." Re-uptake is a natural and normal process, but in depression it can become accelerated. When this occurs, little if any of the neurochemical is available to activate cell "B." After a number of days or weeks, the now abnormally low synaptic levels of these chemicals begin to take their toll. The adjacent cells (cell B) gradually become more and more dysfunctional; this is the second problem. The internal chemistry of the cell changes and even structural elements of the cell may begin to be altered. This heralds the onset of many of the biologic symptoms of depression, as the brain then becomes increasingly ineffective in regulating functions such as sleep and appetite.

If left untreated, this biological malfunction generally does not last forever. In studies of untreated depressed people, it has been noted that a spontaneous reversal of this process and return to normal functioning can take place. Generally this takes place in anywhere from nine to eighteen months. However, obviously this is a very long time to have to suffer with a depression. Fortunately these biological malfunctions can be very successfully treated with proper antidepressant medications.

Also as noted earlier, during severe and prolonged episodes of depression, damage can occur to certain parts of the limbic system (most notably, a brain structure called the *hippocampus*). The main culprit appears to be toxic levels of the stress hormone, cortisol. Such brain damage ultimately can contribute to increasingly severe symptoms and more frequent episodes. Antidepressant medications have been shown to reduce *cortisol* levels. In addition, these drugs increase the availability of a molecule called *brain-derived neurotropic factors* (BDNF). This is a molecule that is manufactured inside nerve cells that helps to facilitate repair of damaged nerve cells and can ignite a process called *neurogeneses* (the birth of new nerve cells to replace those damaged by cortisol).

Unfortunately the effects of antidepressant medications are not rapid. In most cases, a person started on an antidepressant medication will take from ten to twenty-one days to first notice improvement in symptoms. It simply takes that long to start reversing the biological malfunction. Although some antidepressant medications have a built-in sedative effect and thus may help a severe sleep disturbance during the few days of treatment, total resolution of sleep disturbance may take a few weeks. All in all, antidepressant medications have been shown to be quite effective in seventy to eighty percent of properly diagnosed cases. Such treatment can help considerably to ease a number of painful depressive symptoms.

What to Expect

It is very important to have reasonable expectations about medication treatment. Actual responses to medications vary immensely but Jerry H. is a fairly typical example.

Jerry is a forty-one-year-old man who has been married for thirteen years. During the past three years, Jerry and his wife have had considerable marital problems. Last month his wife asked for a divorce and left him. The breakup was very painful to him, and he misses his wife. In the four weeks since she left, Jerry has developed the symptoms noted in Figure 15-B.

Jerry saw a psychiatrist who prescribed an antidepressant medication. The doctor told him to start the medication that night with one 15-mg pill at bedtime. The next day he felt extremely fatigued and groggy and called the doctor. The doctor switched him to a less-sedating medication; the starting dose was one 10-mg pill at bedtime. When the new antidepressant proved to cause no side effects, Jerry was told to increase the dose to 20-mg. after the first week in order to achieve a dose in the therapeutic range. His doctor told him to stay at this dose and to continue taking the same amount each day, since antidepressant medications are effective only when taken on a regular basis. (Please see Figure 15-C for a list of common antidepressant medications and typical therapeutic dosage ranges.)

Figure 15-B

Jerry H.

Psychological Symptoms	*Biological Symptoms*
1. Sadness, crying spells	1. Sleep disturbance; waking up at 4:30 a.m. and unable to go back to sleep.
2. Some social withdrawal	2. Appetite loss; eight pound weight loss
3. Feelings of inadequacy	3. Daytime fatigue; feeling exhausted
	4. Little ability to derive pleasure from normal life activities (anhedonia)

Some antidepressant medications can be sedating and the first medication caused Jerry too much daytime drowsiness. As there are many types of antidepressants, Jerry was wise to call the doctor when he experienced undesirable side effects. In most cases another medication that causes few or no side effects can be prescribed.

Fourteen days after starting to take the medication, Jerry began to notice some gradual changes. He was starting to sleep through the night and he had more energy during the day. Over the next three weeks Jerry noticed that his appetite improved, and he began again to get some enjoyment out of activities like going to the movies or going out to eat with a friend. Also he reported, "I still feel very sad about the divorce, but I don't feel quite so overwhelmed. I still cry at times, but I don't break down at work like I did right after she left me."

The important points I want to make in this example are:

- Medication side effects can occur.
- Most side effects can be dealt with by a change in medications or dosage.
- Changes take a while — the changes may not be noticeable at first.
- Medications can treat the biological aspects of depression and improve emotional control and they have *some* impact on psychological symptoms (but the major effect of medication treatment is to normalize biological functioning).

Two months after beginning treatment, Jerry said, "I still miss my wife a lot, but it's a heck of a lot easier to cope with things now. Being able to sleep, not feeling exhausted, and again being able to feel alive make a big difference." The problems of sadness, low self-esteem, and social withdrawal were not directly affected by the medication. Jerry had to let himself grieve over the loss of his wife while using some cognitive techniques to combat feelings of low self-esteem and inadequacy.

At the end of two and one-half months of treatment, Jerry was fully recovered. Some occasional sadness persisted, but it was not overwhelming. Other depressive symptoms had disappeared. Jerry naturally wanted to stop taking the medication. His therapist, however, suggested he keep taking it for an additional six months. Studies have shown that if people who have been taking medications discontinue the medications as soon as symptoms disappear — even if they are fully recovered — there is a high risk of acute relapse. Most psychiatrists will suggest continued treatment for an additional six to nine months to dramatically reduce the acute relapse rate.

Common Antidepressant Side Effects

Figure 15-C (see page 117) lists currently available antidepressants. Those marked with an asterisk (*) are commonly called "new generation antidepressants." Unlike first generation/older drugs, these newer medications are significantly safer and generally have a much more favorable side effect profile. Side effects vary from drug-to-drug; however, the most common side effects are:

- Nausea, intestinal gas, diarrhea
- Anxiety (most antidepressants significantly reduce anxiety over time, however, some initially increase anxiety or restlessness. If this occurs it typically is noticeable during the first seven to ten days, and then subsides)
- Sexual dysfunction: impotency is rare, but twenty to thirty percent of people taking antidepressants experience *inorgasmia* (difficulty experiencing an orgasm, even though a person is sexually aroused). There is a lower incidence of inorgasmia with Serzone and it is rare with Wellbutrin.
- As depression lifts appetite can improve (i.e., return to normal) and one may gain weight. However, weight gain as a *side effect* is rare during the first few months of treatment (one exception is Remeron that can cause weight gain early in treatment). However, about one out of ten people can have weight gain as a *late-emerging side effect* with many of the other available antidepressants, after taking the medication for a year or more.
- Sedation can occur (see Figure 15-C for specific drugs that may cause this side effect)
- Antidepressants may provoke mania in people who suffer from bipolar disorder (see chapter 17).

If One Medication Does Cause Side Effects, Is it Possible to Switch to Another Which Does Not Bother Me?

Almost any type of medication can cause side effects in some individuals. (Common side effects of antidepressant medications are listed in Figure 15-C.) Some side effects are very minimal and disappear in a few weeks. However, if you do experience significant side effects, it is very important to contact your therapist or physician right away. Many very depressed people who are in need of treatment decide, "This medication doesn't agree with me . . . I'm not going to take drugs," and they discontinue. It is very rare that a medication that has few or no side effects *cannot* be found, although the process may require trials with a few different medications. People who are being treated on the *right* medication do *not* feel drugged, and in fact do not experience any more side effects than one would if taking vitamins. Don't let one unpleasant experience with one medication stop you from getting the help you deserve. You absolutely have the right to discuss any side effect problems with the treating doctor.

What Happens When Medications Do Not Work?

Sometimes medications do not work. There are several common reasons why this could happen:

1. *People are often treated with tiny doses.* Generally speaking you must take medications that are at doses within the therapeutic range (See Figure 15-C). Often, a psychiatrist will prescribe an antidepressant at a very low beginning dose, which is then gradually increased. This is done because gradual increases in dosage can help the body adjust and often avoid side effects.

2. *Many people do not stay on medications long enough.* It is not uncommon to find someone who has taken an antidepressant for one week and decided "This isn't working!" — not understanding that it generally takes two to four weeks (or longer) to begin producing positive results. The person has discontinued the medication before it could be effective.

3. *Depressed people are often given tranquilizers.* Tranquilizers do not cure depression and sometimes make it worse. (See Figure 15-D for a list of commonly prescribed tranquilizers.

4. *Alcohol use/abuse:* Even moderate daily consumption of alcohol can interfere with the action of antidepressants, and this is a very common reason for treatment failures.

5. *The antidepressant chosen may not be effective.* There are five basic classes of antidepressants that differ chemically: Serotonergic antidepressants (often referred to as "SSRI's"); norepinephrine antidepressants; dual action antidepressants (e.g., Eflexor which targets norepinephrine and serotonin); monoamine oxidase inhibitors ("MAOI's") and bupropion (an antidepressant in a class of its own — unlike other antidepressants). Each class of medications affects a unique set of nerve cells in the brain. If someone does not respond to one class of antidepressants, the psychiatrist will switch to a different class, which will probably then be effective.

An effective strategy in common use these days is to "augment" medications — adding a second medication to the first antidepressant. This strategy is often very successful; more than fifty percent of non-responders to the first antidepressant do feel positive benefits. Common medications in use to augment antidepressants include lithium, Wellbutrin, Provigil, Ritalin, or thyroid hormone added to SSRI's.

6. *The depression may be purely psychological.* As mentioned earlier, most cases of psychological depression are not helped by antidepressant medications. There are some exceptions to this and occasionally a psychiatrist will give a trial of antidepressants to people with psychological depressions.

Antidepressant medications do not treat all aspects of clinical depression. In the vast majority of *properly diagnosed* biological depressions, such medications are tremendously effective. The medications are not crutches, but rather a medical intervention that corrects a bio-chemical malfunction and restores normal physiological functioning. As one of my patients recently reported, "As you know, I was very skeptical about taking drugs. I wanted to lick this depression on my own. I know now that I've had to come to terms with most of my problems all on my own. But I also know that there really was something wrong with me physically. The medication did help a lot."

Brief Notes on Over-the-Counter Products

Three over the counter (O.T.C.) products have been shown to be effective antidepressants: These include St. John's Wort (effective in treating some forms of mild-to-moderate depression), SAM-e (effective in treating major depression), and Omega-e fatty acids. Recent research has demonstrated that the dietary supplement EPA (a type of Omega-3 fatty acid available in health food stores) may reduce the severity of major depression (especially when combined with antidepressants). The recommended dose is 0.5 grams, twice a day. (Note: Omega-3 derived from fish oil appears to be more effective than that derived from flax seed oil).

Caution! Despite established efficacy, some O.T.C. products can cause potential serious drug-drug interactions (especially St. John's Wort). *Never* take them along with other antidepressants and *always* tell your doctor that you are taking these O.T.C. products.

Prozac

Prozac is the world's top-selling antidepressant. To date, it is estimated that more than 325 million prescriptions of this medication have been sold, world-wide.

As you're probably aware, Prozac has received a lot of media attention — both positive and negative. The drug was released in the U.S. in 1988 and quickly gained attention, popularity and a reputation as a remarkably safe, well-tolerated and effective treatment for depression. In the early 1990's, however, Prozac suddenly came under fire as accusations were made that use of the drug resulted in cases of suicide and aggressive behavior.

One major source of criticism of Prozac, it was ultimately learned, was the Church of Scientology, which had organized an effective anti-Prozac campaign that contributed much to the negative media blitz. Scientology already had quite a reputation for its ongoing twenty-year war with psychiatry; apparently the organization had decided to focus attention on Prozac.

Frightened patients, skeptical doctors and concerned consumer groups put pressure on the U.S. Food and Drug Administration to carefully review Prozac's safety. After a careful analysis of clinical and research data released in 1991, the FDA concluded that the available information did not indicate that Prozac causes suicidality or violent behavior.

Let's take a look at the facts:

• All medications have side effects.

• Research has shown that newer-generation antidepressants (e.g., Prozac, Zoloft, Wellbutrin) have considerably fewer adverse effects than older generation tricyclic antidepressants (e.g., amitriptyline, imipramine).

• The newer drugs are easier to tolerate and much safer (in cases of accidental or intentional overdose).

• For *all* antidepressants, about two to three percent of people treated report increased thoughts about suicide during the first two weeks of treatment. (Please note: two to three percent report suicidal *thoughts,* not suicidal *behavior.)*

• All antidepressants require two to four weeks of treatment before symptoms begin to improve. Thus, the noted increase in suicidal ideas likely occurred prior to the onset of medication effects.

- There have been cases of individuals committing suicide while taking Prozac and other antidepressants. However, the incidence of this is no greater for those treated with Prozac than those receiving other antidepressants.
- It's unclear whether those isolated cases of suicide (while taking Prozac) are at all related to the drug, or simply a result of depression that had not yet responded to treatment.
- Untreated major depression, tragically, has a ten percent lifetime mortality rate from suicide. Thus it is clear that *untreated* depression carries a statistically greater suicide risk than that of *any* medication treatment, including Prozac. (Of course, such a statistical generalization cannot be applied with certainty to any individual case.)
- Highly-touted new medications that appear to have great promise (like Prozac) often tend to be over-prescribed by busy doctors, particularly for patients who demand a "fast" cure.

Fear or concern are natural reactions to media reports of negative outcomes from any treatment. Such fears are understandable, but it's also important to make a distinction between sensational "horror stories" and actual fact. Approach all medication treatments carefully, following these steps:

1. Study the facts about medications prescribed for you (for *any* condition).

2. Discuss with your physician possible side effects and interactions with other substances or medications you may be taking — including alcohol.

3. Assure yourself that your doctor has prescribed only after thorough examination and diagnosis. Do not push for a "quick cure," no matter how painful the disease. Time is almost always on your side.

4. It is always important that both patient and doctor monitor reactions and side effects very carefully to be certain that the desired results are achieved with a minimum of undesirable effects.

5. Any and all medication side effects should be reported immediately to your physician. Almost always these can be managed by altering the dosage or switching to a different medication.

Prozac and other newer antidepressants are not "magic bullets" to cure depression. However, these medical treatments can be powerful tools when appropriately prescribed and carefully monitored.

Brief Notes on E.C.T. (Electro-convulsive Therapy)

E.C.T., commonly known as "shock therapy," has a history of controversy. The technique was originally developed in the late 1930s, and it found wide use in mental hospitals in the '40s and '50s. Early methods of administering E.C.T. were found to be effective treatments for severe depression, but results were often confounded by significant adverse side effects — such as severe motor convulsions and broken bones — which led to a popular view of E.C.T. as an inhumane form of treatment. Indeed, the idea of intentionally shocking a human being — even if it is clear that the treatment will help in the long run — is repulsive to many people.

Major improvements in E.C.T. came about in the 1970s and '80s, however. The approach is now painless and quite safe. Moreover, E.C.T. is now considered by many professionals to be the most effective treatment for severe depressive disorders. E.C.T. is believed to cause the same beneficial neurochemical changes in the brain as do antidepressant medications — but much more rapidly. The procedure is expensive, however, and therefore is generally used only if psychotherapy and/or medications fail to work adequately.

Brief Notes on New, Experimental Treatments

Two promising treatments have emerged at the turn of the century, that appear to be effective in treating cases of depression that have not responded to more traditional therapies. The first is repetitive transcranial magnetic stimulation. This apparently very safe treatment involves the stimulation of the brain by powerful electromagnets. Preliminary studies suggest that it may be equal in efficacy to E.C.T. However, it has few if any side effects.

The second experimental treatment is called *vagus nerve stimulation*. A pacemaker-like device is implanted in the upper chest, and delivers periodic, low-level electrical stimulation to the vagus nerve that runs through the neck (a nerve that enters the brain). Initial studies are promising, although more research is needed to fully evaluate this procedure.

Brief Notes on Medication Treatment for Children

Many children experience sadness and mild depressions in response to a host of difficult life circumstances. Beyond this, a significant number of youngsters each year also experience very severe depressions (yearly prevalence: 3 percent for children and 10 percent for teenagers). These early onset, severe depressions are frequently the precursors for more severe mood episodes. (Among children and adolescents who suffer from a major depression and are followed for ten years, 35 percent go on to have subsequent depressions, and a staggering 50 percent develop bipolar illness). Antidepressant medication treatment can be helpful in promoting recovery from these serious depressive episodes. However, research on the use of antidepressants in children is fairly limited. The following are important points to note regarding medical treatments:

• Antidepressants can aggravate bipolar disorder (causing "cycle acceleration"; see chapter 17). Since 50 percent of severe childhood depressions ultimately turn out to be the first stages of bipolar illness, treatment with antidepressants must be approached cautiously. However, it is often difficult to tell if an episode of depression in a child is the precursor of bipolar illness. One of the most important things to ascertain is whether or not there is a positive family history of bipolar illness (in blood relatives, and especially in a parent or sibling). This genetically transmitted disorder is frequently seen to run in families. The picture is more clear with relatives who have been diagnosed or treated for bipolar disorder. However, it is often difficult to determine if relatives have had a specific psychiatric disorder. Thus if family members have any of the following, a diagnosis of bipolar disorder is a *possibility*:

- Multiple marriages
- Starting numerous businesses
- Committed suicide
- Severe drug abuse or alcoholism problems

• If bipolar disorder has been ruled out and antidepressant medications are being considered, be aware of the following:

- SSRI's (such as Prozac, Paxil and Zoloft) have the most research support as safe and effective treatments for depression in children and teenagers

- Doses used to treat children often are similar to adult doses (the reason is that pre-pubertal children have a high rate of liver metabolism and when drugs are taken, a significant amount of the medication is metabolized in the liver, resulting in lower blood levels of the drug. Thus higher (i.e., adult) doses are often necessary in order to achieve adequate blood levels of the medication).

- Unfortunately, it often generally takes much longer for antidepressants to begin reducing symptoms in young people (not infrequently eight to twelve weeks). Thus it is very important to be patient and stick with treatment until drug effects are evident.

- Antidepressants are not habit forming.

Medication Treatment for Bipolar Disorder

Please see chapter 17.

Recommended dosages for all medications listed on the following two pages are dose ranges for adults (ages sixteen to sixty). They are presented accurately in accordance with current standards, to the best of the author's knowledge. However, they are not meant to serve as a guide for prescription of medications. Physicians, please check the manufacturer's product information sheet or the *Physician's Desk Reference* for any changes in dosage schedule or contraindications.

Figure 15-C
Common Antidepressant Medications

Generic	Brand	Daily Therapeutic Dosage Range	Sedation	ACH Effects[1]
Names				
Imipramine	Tofranil	150-300 mg	mid	mid
Desipramine	Norpramin	150-300 mg	low	low
Amitriptyline	Elavil	150-300 mg	high	high
Nortriptyline	Aventyl, Pamelor	75-125 mg	mid	mid
Protriptyline	Vivactil	15-40 mg	mid	mid
Trimipramine	Surmontil	100-300 mg	high	mid
Doxepin	Sinequan, Adapin	150-300 mg	high	mid
Clomipramine	Anafranil	150-250 mg	high	high
Maprotiline	Ludiomil	150-225 mg	high	high
Amoxapine	Asendin	150-400 mg	mid	mid
Trazodone	Desyrel	150-400 mg	high	low
Fluoxetine *	Prozac, Sarafem	20-80 mg	low	none
Bupropion, SR*	Wellbutrin, SR	150-400 mg	low	none
Sertraline*	Zoloft	50-200 mg	low	none
Paroxetine*	Paxil, Paxil-CR	20-50 mg	low	low
Venlafaxine X.R.*	Effexor XR	75-350 mg	low	none
Nefazodone*	Serzone	100-500 mg	mid	none
Fluvoxamine*	Luvox	50-300 mg	low	none
Mirtazapine*	Remeron	15-45 mg	mid	low
Citalopram*	Celexa	10-60 mg	low	mid
Escitalopram*	Lexapro	5-20 mg	low	none
Duloxetine	Cymbalta	20-80mg	low	none
Atomoxetine	Strattera	60-120 mg	low	none
Reboxetine*	Vestra	4-8 mg	low	low
Phenelzine[2]	Nardil	30-90 mg	low	none
Tranylcypromine[2]	Parnate	20-60 mg	low	none
Hypericum[3]	St. John's Wort	600-1800 mg	none	none
SAM-e[4]	SAM-e	400-1600 mg	none	none

[1]ACH Effects (anti-cholinergic side effects) Include: dry mouth, constipation, difficulty in urinating and blurry vision.

[2]MAOI (MAO-Inhibitors). Unique class of medications. These require a strict adherence to dietary and medication regime.

[3]This over-the-counter herbal product has some research support of effectiveness in treating mild-to-moderate depression. Can cause serious effects if combined with other medications. Always ask your pharmacist or physician if it is safe to take St. John's Wort with any other medication that is prescribed.

[4]This over-the-counter product has some research support of effectiveness in treating depression. It must be taken with a vitamin-B supplement. SAM-e is the abbreviation for S-adenosylmethionine.

*"New generation" antidepressant medications.

Figure 15-D

Minor Tranquilizers[1]

Names: Tranquilizers

Generic	Brand
ChLordiazepoxide	Librium
Diazepam	Valium
Oxazepam	Serax
Clorazepate	Tranxene
Prazepam	Centrax
Lorazepam	Ativan
Clonazepam	Klonopin

Names: Sedatives[2]

Generic	Brand
Flurazepam	Dalmane
Temazepam	Restoril
Triazolam	Halcion
Quazepam	Doral
Zolpidem	Ambien
Estazolam	Prosom
Zaleplon	Sonata

Names: AntiPanic Medications

Generic	Brand
Alprazolam	Xanax
Clonazepam	Klonopin
Lorazepam	Ativan

[1] All may be habit -forming.
[2] Sedatives: medication used to treat insomnia.

16

Are Medical Treatments the Only Answer to Biological Depression?

What about your lifestyle? Are there non-medical steps you can take to combat depression? Is it possible to change your "brain chemistry" without medication? The answers to these common questions are encouraging, though not absolute.

Most moderate-to-severe biologic depressions require medication treatment. At the same time, however, there are non-medical approaches that are often helpful in the treatment of milder forms of depression or as an adjunct to treatment by medication or psychotherapy. We'll explore some of them in this chapter.

Mom Was Right! You Need Your Sleep!

As we've seen in previous chapters, a central feature of major depression is sleep disturbance. Almost anyone who has been sleep-deprived or had even a few nights of poor quality sleep will notice four common problems: increased emotional sensitivity, irritability, daytime fatigue, and difficulty concentrating.

We all need adequate sleep to function normally — both mentally and physically. Many experts agree that a number of depressive symptoms may stem from the sleep disturbances that accompany depression. In fact, one of the primary target symptoms that suggests a need for antidepressant medication treatment is sleep disturbance.

But medication is not the only answer to sleeping well. There are non-medical ways people can significantly improve sleep — ways that can often make a noticeable difference in lessening symptoms of depression. Let's examine four actions you can take to improve sleep and to reduce depressive symptoms.

Early to Bed . . .

Human physiology evolved over millions of years. And like our fellow living creatures, a number of basic human biological rhythms and drives have developed in accord with the daily cycles of light and dark. Before the discovery of fire and other sources of artificial light, humans undoubtedly kept daily schedules dictated by sunlight: awake during light hours and asleep when it was dark.

But today's lifestyles often do not follow strict schedules or routines. Job demands, shift work, travel, social activities, even television can disrupt our ancestral traditions of a life pattern dictated by light and dark.

One manifestation of our modern schedules is odd or irregular bedtimes — and erratic sleep schedules can throw off internal biologic clocks (the impact of variable sleep patterns is often seen dramatically in people subject to shift work and jet lag). Such irregularity can cause changes in hormone levels and brain chemistry, resulting in further sleep disturbances, including insomnia. The cycle feeds on itself.

Long-term disruptions of this type can result in changes in what is called *sleep architecture*. Each night we all go through various stages of sleep. (You may have seen films of people in laboratory sleep experiments, connected to wires measuring brain activity as they sleep. There are measurable changes throughout the sleep cycle.) Sleep stages vary between *light sleep* and *deep sleep*. It has been found that depression often dramatically alters sleep architecture and can result in very poor quality sleep — especially a reduction in the amount of time spent in deep sleep.

As simple as it may seem, many people benefit greatly by adopting highly regular sleep schedules (i.e., going to bed and awaking at more or less regular times each night). This action can, within a few weeks, normalize internal biology and improve sleep. Sound too simple? You're not alone in thinking that at first glance. It is simple, but try it anyway. For many people, it works remarkably well.

Catch Some Rays

Yet another biological rhythm involves our amount of exposure to sunlight. Early humans were exposed to outdoor light all day, and dark all night. In modern times, most people spend less than ten percent of their daytime hours outside. We work, play and study indoors. One consequence of taking refuge inside is a dramatic reduction in exposure to bright light. As mentioned in chapter 7, some forms of major depression (e.g., Seasonal Affective Disorder) are due primarily to decreased light exposure. Many researchers also believe that decreased photic (sunlight) stimulation may contribute at least somewhat to other types of depression.

One interesting effect of increasing daytime exposure to bright light is that it may help to improve the quality of sleep. Photic stimulation appears to have an impact on the functioning of the hypothalamus, a brain structure involved in the regulation of sleep cycles. An hour a day of exposure to bright light can often improve sleep and reduce some symptoms of depression. One of the best — and simplest — ways to accomplish this is simply to go outside each day and take a walk!

And that leads us to the next positive action — exercise.

Get Moving

Regular exercise is one of the most important and powerful things you can do to decrease depression. Regular exercise (especially aerobic-level exercise) has been associated with increases of certain brain chemicals — *endorphins* and *serotonin* — both of which can reduce depressive symptoms. Also, exercise has been clearly shown to have a positive impact on — here it is again — sleep.

In my clinical experience, I have treated a few very severely depressed patients who responded poorly to standard medical/psychological procedures but, when they began a program of regular exercise in addition to psychotherapy and medication, turned a corner and showed marked improvement for the first time.

Recent research suggest that the "dose" of exercise necessary to combat depression is thirty minutes, three to four times a week. It is important to be certain that the intensity of exercise required is in keeping with one's fitness level (i.e., for less fit people, walking is fine, while jogging, swimming, or running is appropriate for those who are in better athletic shape). This strategy alone has been shown to reduce depression after two to three months of exercising or it may be a useful adjunct to antidepressant medication treatment and relapse prevention. For a "quick fix", try ten to fifteen minutes of brisk walking (this often can reduce negative thinking, low energy, and depressive mood almost immediately, and the effects can last for sixty to ninety minutes). Daily exercise in the form of three ten-minute periods of exercise may also be preferable to the thirty minutes, three to four times-a-week strategy for this purpose. It is prudent to consult your primary health care professional before beginning any rigorous exercise program, even if the goal is to counter depression.

Most people who are depressed find it very difficult to get started with an exercise program. It's especially hard to do it on your own. However, joining a class or getting into regular exercise with a friend or relative can make getting started easier. Doing so may be one of the single most important actions you can take to combat depression!

Watch What You Drink

Two widely used drugs are notorious for disrupting sleep: alcohol and caffeine. Let's take a closer look at each.

Alcohol: Arguably the most used — and abused — drug in the United States, alcohol can provide a very potent and quick sense of release from physical tension and can promote a temporary feeling of euphoria or relaxation. Many people who are depressed seek the quick relief alcohol provides. While I don't intend to be moralistic about the issues of alcohol use, the evidence clearly shows that the use of alcohol can backfire, especially over a prolonged period of time on a regular basis and in moderate-to-high amounts.

Alcohol, in and of itself, is responsible for tremendous *aggravation* of the symptoms of depression. However, alcohol is a seductive substance; because the immediate result of drinking is relief, the person perceives that the alcohol is helpful. But prolonged use actually results in a change in the neurochemistry of the brain, *increasing* — not relieving — depression. In addition, although a couple of drinks may help one to fall asleep, the alcohol continues to work on one's brain chemistry. One clear result is that, several hours after falling asleep, the drinker may experience "rebound insomnia" — the chemical changes actually wake the person up.

An additional side effect of alcohol is reduced time spent in deep sleep, thus further interfering with much-needed rest.

Avoiding, reducing or eliminating alcohol intake during stressful times is one key self-care action that you can take to improve sleep, and in general to relieve depression. *(Note: If you have been drinking heavily, it is important to know that abrupt discontinuation of alcohol can result in very unpleasant and sometimes dangerous withdrawal. Consult your physician.)*

Caffeine: This widely-used drug is found in some unexpected places: in coffee, of course, and in a host of other substances that people consume, including tea, certain drinks (especially colas), and — horrors! — *chocolate!* Caffeine also hides in a number of pain medications (e.g., Excedrin), and in a number of diet pills.

Like alcohol, caffeine is a seductive drug. As you know, one common physical effect of depression is a sense of fatigue and decreased energy. Caffeine is a potent stimulant and can provide, rather quickly, a sense of improved alertness and energy. Some researchers believe that caffeine even has mild antidepressant effects and is no doubt used by some chronically depressed people to elevate their moods.

Caffeine, like alcohol, can backfire. Studies of caffeine use and abuse indicate that when people ingest more than 250 mg. per day of caffeine (roughly two cups of coffee), there is a significant likelihood of developing such stress-related symptoms as jitteriness, tension, anxiety and insomnia. The risk of symptoms increases dramatically when the amount of caffeine surpasses 500 mg. per day.

Sleep is a factor here too. An often unrecognized but important symptom of caffeine use is disruption of the quality of sleep. Even if you're able to go to sleep, even moderate amounts of caffeine produce significantly more restless sleep. As a result, you'll fail to get adequate rest during the night, which leads to excessive daytime fatigue. To combat this fatigue, the typical coffee/cola drinker chooses — you guessed it — to drink more caffeine.

In difficult times, it may seem silly to worry about the amount of coffee you're drinking. Many people "pooh-pooh" the notion that caffeine contributes to emotional problems, but clinical research shows that caffeine can cause or exacerbate stress-related symptoms, especially sleep disturbances.

The bottom line here: *One decisive action you can take during times of depression is to reduce or eliminate caffeine.* Note that — as with other strong drugs — if you are accustomed to drinking large amounts of caffeine, and you quit "cold turkey," you will likely experience significant caffeine withdrawal symptoms: anxiety, restlessness, tension and headaches. Thus if you have become accustomed to ingesting large amounts of caffeine, you'll want to *gradually* decrease your intake of caffeine over a period of two to three weeks, progressively replacing caffeinated beverages with decaffeinated beverages.

Caffeine Consumption Questionnaire

		Average number of ounces/doses/tablets per day	Average total per day

Beverages

Coffee (6 oz.)	125mg	X _____	=	_____
Decaf Coffee (6 oz.)	5 mg	X _____	=	_____
Tea (with caffeine, 6 oz.)	50 mg	X _____	=	_____
Hot cocoa (6 oz.)	15 mg	X _____	=	_____
Caffeinated Soft Drinks (12 oz.)	40-60 mg	X _____	=	_____
Chocolate candy bar	20 mg	X _____	=	_____

Over-the-Counter Medications

Anacin	32 mg	X _____	=	_____
Appetite-control pills	100-200 mg	X _____	=	_____
Dristan	16 mg	X _____	=	_____
Excedrin	65 mg	X _____	=	_____
Extra Strength Excedrin	100 mg	X _____	=	_____
Midol	132mg	X _____	=	_____
NoDoz	100mg	X _____	=	_____
Triaminicin	30 mg	X _____	=	_____
Vanquish	33 mg	X _____	=	_____
Vivarin	200 mg	X _____	=	_____

Prescription Medications

Cafergot	100 mg	X _____	=	_____
Fiorinal	40 mg	X _____	=	_____
Darvon compound	32 mg	X _____	=	_____

TOTAL MG. CAFFEINE PER DAY   _____

250 milligrams per day *may* interfere with deep sleep

What About Diet?

Are we really what we eat? Questions about diet abound, and it's common to wonder about the effects of diet on emotional health. Research shows that during times of depression people tend to develop poor eating habits. And in the long run, poor nutrition contributes to health problems — including mental health problems.

No doubt about it, diet and health are related. The problem is, we don't yet know exactly *how.* Still, there has been a great deal of active research in recent years and, while the findings are not yet definitive, it is interesting to note some of the results. An impressively comprehensive survey of "nutritional neuroscience" research written by Randy Blaun and published in *Psychology Today* magazine in June 1996, reports a number of findings that may be important to our understanding of depression.

• Cincinnati physician/researcher Charles Glueck notes that a high level of blood cholesterol, particularly triglycerides, is related to depression and manic depression. In fact, Glueck's research shows *that high blood-fat level alone can cause depression,* and reducing fat intake can markedly improve depressive symptoms.

• A number of studies suggest that a radical and sudden *reduction* in dietary cholesterol has been associated with decreased brain serotonin levels, and results in increased irritability and depression. When we consider this in light of Dr. Glueck's findings, obviously the role of dietary fats and mood is complex and not yet fully understood but it does appear that achieving a normal cholesterol level is potentially helpful in combatting depression.

• Carbohydrates may not only help you run faster, they may be important to brain function. Dr. Judith Wurtman of MIT, author of *The Serotonin Solution,* finds that *"carbos" may help alleviate anxiety and depression,* by facilitating the brain's ability to convert tryptophan into serotonin. (You know from the previous chapter — pages 104-106 — that certain chemicals help carry the electrical impulses between brain cells, and you'll recall that serotonin is one such neurochemical; it's a depression fighter.) However, complex carbos are best (e.g., fruits and vegetables). Simple carbohydrates (like sugar and candy bars) result in only very temporary elevations in mood, followed by a crash back into depression, and often lead to weight gain. Sorry.

• Studies at the U.S. Department of Agriculture Human Nutrition Research Center have shown that *severe vitamin B deficiency (e.g., thiamine, folic acid, niacin) can disturb brain function and lead to high levels of anxiety and depression.* Folic acid supplements have produced dramatic relief of symptoms of depression for some patients.

• Protein snacks without carbohydrates can often increase energy, motivation and mental clarity. Protein is best derived from: protein power, tofu, lean meats, or eggs.

• A regular diet rich in omega-3 fatty acids has been shown to reduce intense mood instability in some people. The best source of omega-e fatty acids are fish and other sea foods. Fish oil supplements found in health food stores also provide this fatty acid.

• Dr. Barbara Strupp, associate professor of psychology at Cornell University, confirms what mom always told you: the best way to get the right combination of necessary brain nutrients and depression-fighting neurochemicals is to *eat a balanced diet.* Moreover, says Strupp, "Whether or not you'll sustain a benefit depends on where you start off." If your diet is deficient in key nutrients needed for optimum brain function, adding those elements is more likely to be of help.

• In one of the most telling statements in the *Psychology Today* report, writer Randy Blaun observes that ". . . it would not be prudent to wolf down mega-amounts of vitamins and minerals. Reliable studies of the long-term effects of mega-doses have yet to be done . . ."

• Although the cutting-edge research in nutritional neuroscience holds much promise, *the evidence does not yet strongly support changes in diet alone as an effective way to deal with depression.*

Nevertheless, I have had patients who report that dietary approaches have reduced their depressive symptoms. You may find changes in your diet to be a helpful part of your own efforts to beat depression, but don't rely on diet — or any other approach — alone.

In Sum . . .

The most powerful treatments for depression are psychotherapy and antidepressant medications. Research has made that clear, but there are a number of other approaches that can make a difference, and the suggestions made in this chapter are very helpful for many depressed individuals. And yet, many people who are feeling very discouraged or hopeless find ideas such as reducing caffeine or exercising or eating certain foods so trivial or so unlikely to help, that they won't try them. In waging a war against depression, *you need to pull out all the stops,* and attack it on every possible front. Please consider taking the suggestions in this chapter and putting them into action today! There are no guarantees, but I think you'll find that they *will* help.

17

Bipolar Disorder:
Diagnosis and Treatment

Y ou may be wondering what a chapter called "Bipolar Disorder" is doing in a book on depression. The answer is simpler than you might think. The condition now known as *bipolar disorder* was previously called *manic-depressive* illness. Like depression, it's a mood disorder, and its major symptoms are severe and rapid swings between depression and a state of high activity known as *mania*. Some of the discussion in this chapter may sound a bit technical to you, but it's important to know some details about bipolar disorder as a key part of understanding depression and how to deal with it.

Bipolar disorder is quite common, affecting from three to five percent of the population over the lifespan. According to the U.S. National Institute of Mental Health, "Bipolar disorder (formerly called manic-depressive illness) is a common type of mood disorder affecting between 3.5-5 percent of the population (lifetime prevalence). According to the US National Institute of Mental Health: "Bipolar disorder . . . is a brain disorder that causes unusual shifts in a person's mood, energy, and ability to function. Different from the normal ups and downs that everyone goes through, the symptoms of bipolar disorder are severe. They can result in damaged relationships, poor job or school performance, and even suicide. But there is good news: bipolar disorder can be treated, and people with this illness can lead full and productive lives."

It is now appreciated that there are several different types of bipolar disorder and together these are often referred to as bipolar spectrum disorders. Bipolar disorders are a group of genetically-transmitted illnesses that result in recurring episodes of depression and mania or hypomania (see below). There are life-long disorders which require on-going medical treatment. Mood-stabilizing medications can effectively reduce episode severity and frequency; however there is currently no cure.

Sixty percent of manic episodes are classic manias (see Figure 17-A); forty percent are referred to as dysphoric or mixed mania (see Figure 17-B).

Figure 17-A

Symptoms of Classic Mania

- Euphoria or an inflated sense of self-worth
- Restlessness, agitation, hyperactivity
- High level of energy
- Decreased need for sleep
  (e.g., sleeping three to four hours per night, yet without daytime fatigue)
- Racing thoughts and rapid, pressured speech
- Poor judgement and impulsive behavior, e.g., spending enormous amounts of money, driving fast/recklessly, marked alcohol or drug abuse, promiscuity and engaging in unsafe sex
- Psychotic symptoms can occur

Figure 17-B

Symptoms of Dysphoric or Mixed Mania

- Symptoms in common with classic mania
  - Agitation, restlessness, hyperactivity
  - Decreased need for sleep
  - Racing thoughts and rapid, pressured speech
  - Psychotic symptoms can occur
- Marked irritability
- Negative, pessimistic thinking
- Feelings of worthlessness
- Suicidal ideas

Hypomania is a milder version of mania that typically involves much less intense mood symptoms. Hypomania often lasts only two to four days and is frequently not noticed as being a sign of illness by the person experiencing the symptoms (although most times family members are more clearly aware of the mood changes and increased energy). During some hypomanias the person can feel highly motivated, productive, witty, gregarious, and "up beat" (although there is often underlying irritability). One very common sign of hypomania is a decreased need for sleep with no daytime fatigue.

Three Common Subtypes of Bipolar Disorder

• *Bipolar I:* severe manic (classic or dysphoric) and depressive episodes (often with periods of normal/balanced mood between episodes).

• *Bipolar II:* characterized by frequent, severe and prolonged depressions with periodic, brief episodes of hypomania, a normal/balanced mood can occur between episodes, but often during these in-between times there is a low-grade/mildly depressed mood.

• *Cyclothymia:* mild depressions and hypomania (note: this less severe version of bipolar can become worse with time and *most* people with cyclothymia eventually "convert" to Bipolar I or Bipolar II).

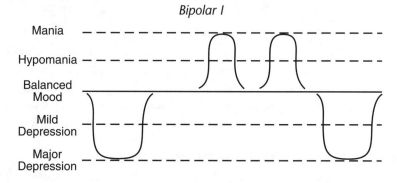

Bipolar I

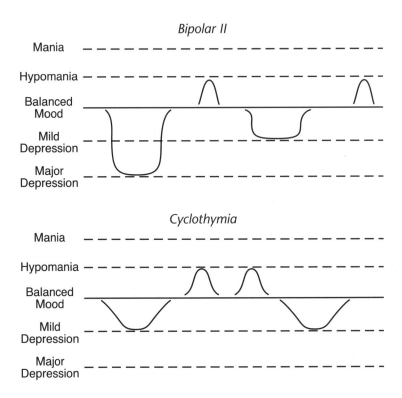

A complication of bipolar disorder affecting about twenty percent of suffers is called *rapid cycling*. This represents a time-limited worsening of the illness, in which episodes occur with greater frequency (i.e., four or more episodes of depression, mania or hypomania per year). Most cases of rapid cycling last a few months to a year-and-a-half and then subside. The most common cause for rapid cycling is substance use or abuse.

Bipolar Disorder Must Be Treated

Untreated or poorly treated bipolar illness leads to disaster. Careers and marriages are ruined, physical health problems abound, and there is a high rate of suicide. If not treated, most cases of bipolar disorder become progressively worse. The sooner this illness can be diagnosed and properly treated, the better.

Treatments for Bipolar Disorder

Treatment must have a two-pronged focus: bringing to an end the current manic or depressive episode *and* relapse prevention. With proper medical treatment most people can experience a marked decrease in episode frequency and severity.

Life-style Management: People with bipolar illness have a very unstable and fragile nervous system and mood episodes can be triggered by a number of environmental and physical stressors. It is especially important for bipolar patients to regulate their lifestyles closely: without this, medical treatments often are only partially effective. Most important are:

• Maintain regular bed times and awakening times. Regular sleep patterns are crucial

• Avoid substance abuse and alcohol abuse like the plague (substance abuse is very common in bipolar disorder and often significantly aggravates the illness)

• Avoid sleep deprivation, shift work and crossing time zones

• Avoid or greatly minimize caffeine use, since it can significantly disrupt the quality of sleep

• Keep the amount of bright light exposure (e.g., sunlight) stable (in terms of time exposed each day) year round.

Medical Treatments: Manic episodes are treated with a variety of medications referred to as *mood stabilizers* (see Figure 17-C). In addition, mania is often treated with minor tranquilizers (see Figure 15-D) and/or *atypical antipsychotics* (see Figure 17-D). Please note that atypical antipsychotic medications certainly do treat psychotic symptoms if they are present, however they have also been found to be effective anti-manic agents, as well. Mood stabilizers often take ten days to begin to reduce manic symptoms, and several weeks longer to truly resolve mania (antipsychotics and minor tranquilizers can often reduce some of the severe agitation seen in manias in a few hours to a few days). Once manic symptoms have abated, mood stabilizers and sometimes atypical antipsychotics will continue to be used to decrease the likelihood of future manic and depressive episodes (this is the mainstay of relapse prevention). Complete relapse prevention is rarely achieved, although on-going medication treatment can *significantly* reduce episode frequency and severity.

Depressive episodes seen in bipolar disorder are often very challenging to treat. Some mood stabilizers have antidepressant effects (especially Lamictal, and possibly Depakote and Lithium) as well as the drug Symbyax (a combination of an antidepressant and antipsychotic).

Antidepressants are also often used in combination with mood stabilizers to treat bipolar depression, although there is some controversy regarding their use. Some evidence exists that antidepressants may aggravate bipolar illness and/or provoke switches from depression into mania or hypomania. If you are being treated with antidepressants, please discuss this issue with your physician (more information about risks for antidepressants in bipolar depression can be found on the National Institute of Mental Health website: www.nimh.nih.gov).

Figure 17-C

Mood Stabilizers

Generic Names	Brand	Daily Therapeutic Dosage Range
Lithium carbonate	Eskalith, Lithonate	600-2400 mg
Carbamazepine	Tegretol	600-1600 mg
Oxcarbazepine	Trileptal	1200-2400 mg
Divalproex	Depakote	750-1500 mg
Gabapentin	Neurontin	300-2400 mg
Lamotrigine	Lamictal	50-500 mg
Topiramate	Topamax	25-300 mg

Figure 17-D

Atypical Antipsychotics

Generic Names	Brand	Daily Therapeutic Dosage Range
Olanzepine	Zyprexa	5-20 mg
Risperidone	Risperdal	2-12 mg
Ziprasidone	Geodon	60-160 mg
Quetiapine	Seroquel	150-400 mg
Aripiprazole	Abilify	15-30 mg
Clozapine	Clozaril[1]	300-900 mg

[1]All of the above mentioned antipsychotic drugs have been developed during the past decade and are significantly safer and better tolerated that early-generation anti-psychotic medications. Clozapine is an exception. It is an older-generation drug that has significant side effects; it is mentioned here because this drug, despite problematic side effects, has been shown to be an excellent anti-manic agent and also is useful in the long-term management of bipolar illness. Owing to its side effects, it is rarely used as an initial treatment, but is an important medication especially in difficult to treat cases.

Seventy percent of people receiving treatment for bipolar illness in the United States are treated with two or more mood stabilizers at the same time. It has been found that such combination therapy is often effective and necessary.

Here are the hard facts: medication treatment *must* continue for a lifetime. Without this, bipolar disorder can quickly become more severe and harder to treat. Yet *most* people with bipolar discontinue medications (against medical advice), and the primary reason is because of side effects. Unfortunately, mood stabilizers are notorious for causing significate side effects. A discussion of the many and varied side effects is beyond the scope of this book. However, please be open and assertive with your prescribing physician regarding side effects problems. Often these can be minimized by a change in medications or dosage adjustments. Patient-initiated discontinuation of mood stabilizers has resulted in many disasters, and this issue must be taken very seriously.

Bipolar Vignette

Sandy is an outgoing, very well-liked and successful twenty-six-year-old math teacher for a local community college. One evening recently she made telephone calls to a number of her students in the middle of the night telling them to come down to her office immediately. Ten of her students did, in fact, show up on campus at 1:00 a.m. to find her in a state of excitement, eager to tell them about a new mathematical equation that she had "discovered" during the past two days. This middle-of-the-night experience caused the students a lot of concern. The next day they learned that their teacher was in the hospital.

After three days in the psychiatric unit of the local hospital, Sandy began to calm down and started to face the reality that she had gone through an incredible week. At first, feeling increasing energy and virtually no need for sleep, she had been elated as her mind raced to tremendous and wildly creative thoughts. She began to believe that she had found a new way of looking at mathematical equations that would somehow change the world. Two days prior to her hospitalization, however, she began to feel more and more agitated and uneasy. Her thoughts continued to race, but she was beginning to feel out of control, and it scared her.

Two weeks after her midnight "class meeting" Sandy was significantly more calm and rational. The medication she was taking was helping her to settle down and to feel like herself again. She was released from the hospital having learned that she had had a manic episode and was suffering from bipolar disorder. She had always been well adjusted, and it frightened her to think that somehow she had lost control in such a profound way. It just didn't seem possible that she could have a mental illness.

Psychotherapy is Crucial Too!

Although medication treatment is the backbone of successful therapy for bipolar disorder, a number of studies have clearly shown that psychotherapy can significantly contribute to better outcomes. Family therapy and psycho-education have been found to be most helpful in the treatment of this condition. *Family therapy* is aimed at helping all members of the patient's family understand more about bipolar disorder. Long-term success in treating bipolar disorder is significantly enhanced if family members truly appreciate the nature of the disorder. It is especially important for them to understand that many of the symptoms are driven by biological changes in brain chemistry, and are not fully under control of the person suffering from the illness. All family members of people with bipolar disorder go through their own hell living with the illness. Mood swings can be devastating to all who love and care about the person with the disorder. A realistic understanding of the illness helps family members to develop a deeper attitude of compassion and to find support and healing for their own emotional pain.

Many mood swings become intensified by stresses in a person's life, and interpersonal conflicts often contribute a good deal to this increased mood instability. Family therapy actively focuses on developing communication and problem-solving skills that can help to reduce such conflicts (see Fast and Preston, 2004).

Psycho-educational therapy is a form of brief therapy which may also involve a spouse or significant other, or the entire family. The focus is on helping everyone understand the symptoms and characteristics of bipolar illness and its treatment. Especially important goals in this approach are to develop of an attitude of compassion toward the patient, and to help family members become experts in recognizing the early, subtle signs of another impending mood swing. Spotted early, many severe mood swings can be nipped in the bud, and often family members can notice these early warning signs even better than the person suffering from bipolar illness.

Individual therapy is also very important in the treatment of bipolar disorder, especially in helping the person come to terms with the harsh reality of having to live with this serious chronic illness. Ultimately this involves grieving the loss of a more stable life, and learning to appreciate and nurture one's own gifts and strengths that can be realized despite bipolar illness.

Additional Resources for Bipolar Disorder

Miklowitz, D.J. (2002) *The Bipolar Disorder Survival Guide,* Guilford Press.

Fast, J. & Preston, J. (2004) *Loving Someone with Bipolar Disorder: How to Help and Understand Your Partner,* New Harbinger Publications.

18

Depression Is A Family Affair

When someone is depressed, often the entire family is affected. This chapter explores some of the common issues that occur for depressed people and their families.

"We Care and We Want To Help"

Many times, the first response to a depression, is for friends and family members to rally around the depressed person, to express caring, and to try to help. In talking to thousands of depressed patients, it is clear that some types of "help" are tremendously supportive, while other types actually make things worse. It is so normal, so natural for people to say: "Everything will be all right," or "It can't be that bad." These comments may reflect good intentions, but such statements do not help. Almost always the depressed person will feel that "They don't really understand" or "How can they know? It is that bad!"

Some statements on first glance sound supportive, but carry a hidden ✓ criticism: "You *shouldn't* feel so upset," "You *should* be over this by now," "You *shouldn't* let it get to you so much." The underlying message is "There is something wrong with you . . . You aren't coping well . . . You should be able to snap out of it." You may recognize these "should statements" as remarks which do not help. If people could simply "snap out of" a depression, they would. Such comments often result in lower self-esteem, which makes a depression worse. A recent patient of mine said, "They are right . . . I shouldn't be so upset. There is just something defective about me." She felt worse.

The problem is that even loving, caring people are frequently ignorant about the process of normal grieving. Many people simply do not understand that it is normal and adaptive to feel and express pain after losses, and that emotional wounds do not quickly heal. And most people who have never experienced depression simply do not understand what it is like to be depressed.

Why Do People Pull Away?

While a depressed person may desire to be alone at times, prolonged isolation is not generally helpful. Just when one may need to maintain contact with others, friends and family often shy away. How come? Mainly because it's hard to be around someone who is depressed, for several reasons. It is often very painful to experience someone else's sorrow or grief. Such emotions can touch upon similar feelings in ourselves. In addition, many are at a loss for words, don't know what to say, and are fearful of unintentionally upsetting their friends. It can be very frustrating to be around someone who has been depressed for a long time. Frustration and guilt can lead to irritability and increase the distance in a relationship. A spouse and other loved ones may pull away, and the depressed person feels even more alone when family members do not understand about depression.

Aaron Kennedy is a forty-one-year-old businessman whose wife has had recurring serious problems with depressions during the past five years. He came to me to talk about his feelings regarding his wife's depression:

"I honestly love my wife. We've had a good life together. And I feel very sorry for her when she feels depressed. But I'm just getting worn-out. I keep trying to support her. I tell her I love her and that things will get better, but she keeps looking so depressed. Sometimes I try to get her to snap out of it, to just go with me for a drive in the country. She feels so tired and won't go, and I feel so damned angry at her. I feel like saying 'What's wrong with you? Why don't you just try?' But I feel guilty because I know she can't help it."

So What Can a Family Do?

One important step is for relatives to *get information about depression.* While there may be a lot that depressed persons can do to assist themselves, no one is able to magically "snap-out-of-it." Depression is a time of emotional paralysis. Family and friends often believe that their loved ones could help themselves "if only they would." That notion is a myth. If family members can come to understand how a depression's grip can be very difficult to shake, it may be much easier for them to accept and tolerate the depression.

A second thing that helps is to *show acceptance for the depressed person's feelings.* Let the person know "I know you're hurting," but don't try to talk someone out of the bad feeling. It's not appropriate or healthy to assume responsibility for trying to cure someone's depression. A friend or family member certainly can provide support, caring and encouragement, but it is a tremendous burden to feel that "I *need* to cheer him up." It's extremely hard to do, and "cheering up" rarely helps the person who is feeling depressed. One of my men patients, who lost his son in an automobile accident, recently said to me:

"I get so tired of people trying to cheer me up. But the other day one of my friends said something to me that helped more than anything. He said, 'Sam, I know this has been killing you. I feel bad. I love you Sam. I want you to know I'm here if you need me.' I felt like he really understood."

Let's look at this statement. Sam's friend did not tell him what he "should feel." Rather, the friend honestly acknowledged Sam's feelings. Next, he told Sam how he felt seeing his friend in such pain. And finally he said, "I'm here if you need me." This last point is important. Times of depression are times of tremendous loneliness, and it helps considerably to maintain contact with others.

In a nutshell, an appropriate caring and supportive message could say, "I know you are hurting. I care about how you feel. I'm available."

Reassurance may not be enough, however. If your friend or loved one has become immobilized by apathy, fatigue, and hopelessness, it is very important to *encourage a visit with a mental health professional* or family doctor.

Finally, you may help your depressed relative if you *take care of yourself.* You have needs and feelings which must not be overlooked. It's okay for you to experience some fun even if the depressed person does not. Also you must learn to acknowledge your feelings of frustration, irritation, and despair; otherwise, you may be overwhelmed as well. In therapy, Aaron Kennedy became increasingly aware of his frustrations about his depressed wife. In fact she had sensed his resentment and actually felt better when he finally was honest with her. It helps to be candid about such feelings, and to avoid blaming the other person. It may be helpful for *all* family members to talk jointly with a therapist about how they are feeling. Your ability to be supportive can continue only as long as you look after some of your own needs and feelings.

Family members, particularly those who live with the depressed person, inevitably play some part in a depression. Sensitive concern for the loved one's feelings, availability when needed, and avoidance of an unrealistic "cheer up" attitude can be of genuine help.

Advice to Friends or Family Members of Depressed Loved Ones Who Refuse to Seek Treatment

The hopelessness and pessimism that is such a central feature in depression often are at the root of reluctance to seek professional help. Pleading with a depressed relative to get treatment sometimes falls on deaf ears. And this can be terribly upsetting for others who have to witness on-going suffering and feel helpless to convince the depressed person to get help.

To complicate matters, stubbornness and shame often are underlying factors that result in a refusal to get treatment. Self-reliance and a "pull yourself up by your boot-straps" mentality, unfortunately, are fostered in our culture. Yet the facts are clear. Almost no one can simply "snap out of" a depression. And this has nothing to do with one's intellect, will power, or overall strength of character.

Hopefully the following may be helpful suggestions to share with a friend or relative who refuses to get help:

Here are the facts:

• Serious depression ultimately affects one out of six people.

• Depression strikes even very bright, strong competent people (for example, consider such men as Churchill and Lincoln, who suffered from depression.)

• No amount of encouragement alone can bring someone out of depression . . . "cheer up . . . look at the bright side of life. . . snap out of it." You know it's true; ultimately, such advice really does not help.

• Untreated, depression generally lasts twelve months or longer. It can last for years.

• Depression typically gets worse before it gets better.

• Depression can ruin marriages and careers.

• More than eighty percent of people who get appropriate treatment make a good recovery.

• Seeking treatment is a safe, low-risk experiment. Please consider this: what do you have to lose by going to therapy for a period of at least one month? Give it a try and then you be the judge.

And finally, to get treatment is to take action (rather than to passively submit). It is an act of kindness toward yourself — and very importantly, it may be one of the most important things you ever do for the sake of your loved ones.

19

There Is Hope!

To feel discouraged or hopeless when one is depressed is a very common experience.

In this book I have discussed both self-help approaches and professional treatment. For the vast majority of depressed adults these approaches are very successful. When you're feeling stuck or unmotivated, however, it's hard to get started helping yourself. If you wait to feel motivated before you take action, you may be waiting for a long time. Take some action *now*, even if the energy or motivation is not there.

If you are feeling depressed, it is important either to begin using *the self-help strategies,* or to *call and make an appointment with a therapist.* I know that this is sometimes tremendously difficult to do. In fact, getting started — just doing *something* — can feel like an impossible task. Maybe you'd find it easier to confide in a close friend or relative as a first step. You could say something like this: "I've been feeling depressed. I know I have to do something about it, but I'm having trouble getting started. I need your help." You can then ask the friend/relative to help and encourage you. This person could, in a sense, keep you "on track," making sure you do such things as calling and making an appointment with a therapist or beginning to use some cognitive techniques on a daily basis. The support of a friend might be just what you need to help you take that first difficult step. Call somebody! It is extremely valuable to maintain contact with others when you feel depressed.

One of my patients recently said, "I had been so depressed for months. I kept thinking that I shouldn't feel so bad and that I should just snap out of it. I'd feel a little better, but it didn't last very long, and I just felt worse and worse. I don't know why I waited so long to get therapy. What finally made the difference was telling my best friend. She listened, then said, 'Get some help.' Now, I wish I had come to see you sooner."

Saying "I shouldn't be feeling so bad" rarely helps. You either do feel bad or you don't. The important point is to call to make an appointment, or to enter treatment, or to try some self-help work, or to do something active to come out of the depression. Taking action is crucial. Even though no single remedy can put an immediate stop to depression, taking that first step can leave you feeling a little less helpless. Action is an antidote for feelings of powerlessness.

I hope that one message has been clear throughout this book. We are all human beings, and it's human to feel hurt when we confront loss and disappointment. Life is often hard, and sometimes it's tragic. Thank goodness, however, there are ways to deal with emotional pain, to grieve for our losses, and to heal. Even in the face of what seems like overwhelming despair, it is possible for you to beat depression and recover — to become able to feel alive again.

So get moving and *do something* about it!

I wish you well.

References/
Index

References

Beck, A.T. (1976) *Cognitive Therapy and the Emotional Disorders,* The New American Library Inc., New York.

Burns, D.D. (1999) *Feeling Good, The New Mood Therapy,* HarperCollins Publishers., New York.

Burns, D.D. (1985) *Feeling Good About Yourself,* Psychology Today Tapes, American Psychological Association, Washington, D.C.

Duveneck, M.J., Portwood, M.M., Wicks, J.J. & Lieberman, J.S. (1986) Depression in Myotonic Muscular Dystrophy. *Archives of Physical Medicine and Rehabilitation,* Vol. 67, pp. 875-877.

Fast, J. & Preston, J. (2004) *Loving Someone with Bipolar Disorder: How to Help and Understand Your Partner,* New Harbinger Publications, Oakland, California.

Kushner, H.S. (1986) *When All You've Ever Wanted Isn't Enough,* Pocket Books, New York.

Lewisohn, P.M. & Graf. M. (1973) Pleasant activities and depression. *Journal of Consulting and Clinical Psychology,* 41: 261-268.

Mark, R. (1999) *Bipolar Disorder: A Guide for Patients and Families.*

Osterweis, M., Solomon, F., & Green, M. (Eds.) (1984) *Bereavement: Reactions, Consequences and Care,* National Academy Press. Washington, D.C.

Preston, J. (2001) *Depression and Anxiety Management* (Audio Tape), New Harbinger Publications, Oakland, California.

Preston, J.D. & Johnson, J.R. (2004) *Clinical Psychopharmacology Made Ridiculously Simple,* MedMaster, Inc., Miami, Florida.

Preston, J.D., O'Neal, J. & Talaga, M. (2000) *Consumer's Guide to Psychiatric Drugs,* New Harbinger Publications, Oakland, California.

Time Magazine, (1986) Talk is as Good as a Pill: NIMH study shows psychotherapy lifts depression, 60.

Other Recommended Books

Beck, A.T., Rush, A.J., Shaw, B.F. & Emery, G. (1979) *Cognitive Therapy of Depression,* The Guilford Press, New York.

Beckfield, D. (2004) *Master Your Panic* (Third Edition), Impact Publishers, Atascadero, California.

Boenisch, E. & Haney, C.M. (2003) *Stress Owners Manual* (Second Edition), Impact Publishers, Atascadero, California.

Butler, P.E. (1981) *Talking to Yourself: Learning to Communicate Wlth the Most Important Person In Your Life,* Stein and Day, New York.

Fiere, R. (1975) *Mood Swings,* Bantam Books, Toronto.

Gold, M.S. (1986) *The Good News About Depression,* Bantam Books, Toronto.

Greist, J.H. & Jefferson, J.W. (1984) *Depression and its Treatment: Help for the Nation's #1 Mental Problem,* American Psychiatric Press, Inc., Washington, D.C.

Kushner, H.S. (1980) *When Bad Things Happen To Good People,* Avon Books, New York.

Preston, J. (1996) *Life Is Hard* (Audio Tape), Impact Publishers, Atascadero, California.

Stearns, A.K. (1984) *Living Through Personal Crisis,* Ballantine Books, New York.

Index

low self-, 15–16
self-, depression checklist, 25
events, realistic vs. distorted
    response to painful (fig.), 70
exercise and avoiding depression,
    121–122
existential crises, 36–38

–F–

failure
    and the apathy cycle, 89
    childhood experiences of, 34
    and low self-esteem, 38
family
    counselors, 101
    helping depressed members of,
        138–139
    history of depression, suicide,
        alcoholism, 18–19
    harsh environments, 32–33
family therapy, 134
fatigue, 18, 24
fear, childhood experiences of, 31
feelings
    accepting depressed persons',
        139–141
    in cognitive therapy, 66–68
    expressing and accepting, 64
    of perceived helplessness, 95
fish oil supplements, 126
food
    appetite disturbances, 18
    diet and depression, 125–126
Frost, Robert, 82
frustration (depression checklist), 26

–G–

Glueck, Charles, 125
grief
    and the apathy cycle, 89
    in early childhood, 31
    normal process of, 36
    suppressing, 62
    vs. depression, 6
growth hormone, 18
guilt and depression, 16

–H–

headache medications and depression
    (fig.), 42
healing
    actions which block emotional
        (fig.), 63
    actions which promote emotional
        (fig.), 64
    by challenging cognitive distortions,
        82
helplessness and emotional stress, 45
herbal antidepressants, 117
high-blood fat and depression, 125
high blood pressure and sleep
    disturbances, 43–44
hippocampus, 106
history
    family, 18–19
    personal, 29–34
hopelessness, 57–58
hormonal changes
    and biological depression, 44
    and depression, 6, 11, 18
hormones
    and depression (fig.), 42
    stress, 106
    TSH (thyroid stimulating hormone),
        43
hypersomnia, 17
hypochondria, 19
hypomania, 129
hypothalmus, 41, 47, 104
hypothyroidism, 43

–I–

illness
    and biological depression, 43
    as cause of depression, 38–39
    and depression, 11–12
immune system
    and depression, 6
    and hypothalmus, 41
individual therapy, 135
infidelity, self-help cognitive therapy
    for, 78–81
inorgasmia, 109
insomnia, 17, 122

More Healing Resources
by Dr. John Preston

Survivors: *Stories and Strategies*
to Heal the Hurt
John Preston, Psy.D.
Softcover: $15.95   288 pages
Forget TV. Forget desert islands and remote
jungles. This book offers *real* help for *real*
emotional issues, through the stories of four
ordinary people, each going through a very
painful life experience, each plagued by
significant emotional despair. Fortunately, they
all share one vitally important human quality: an inherent capacity to
heal from deep emotional wounds. They are Survivors.

This remarkable book presents nine proven strategies to help them
through their plights, combining the best of storytelling, self-help, and
professional guidance, bringing readers an unparalleled resource for
overcoming emotional pain.

Dr. Preston's outstanding reputation as a therapist, teacher, lecturer,
and author are well-earned, and the reasons are obvious in this
uplifting, practical, readable work.

Life Is Hard: *An Audio Guide to Healing Emotional Pain*
Audiocassette, 60 minutes $11.95
John Preston, Psy.D.
In a very warm and highly personal style, psychologist Preston
offers listeners powerful advice — realistic, practical, effective —
on dealing with the emotional pain life inflicts upon us. Based on the
best current psychological knowledge and procedures. Avoid
unnecessary pain by gaining control over your reactions.

More Books With *Impact*

We think you will find these Impact Publishers titles of interest:

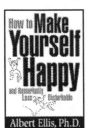

How to Make Yourself Happy and Remarkably Less Disturbable
Albert Ellis, Ph.D.
Softcover: $15.95   224 pages
Rid yourself of disturbing thoughts, anxiety, depression, rage, self-hate, self-pity. Self-help action steps + real-life case examples + witty, articulate style = practical wisdom from one of the most highly-respected psychologists of our time.

The Stress Owner's Manual: Meaning, Balance *and Health in Your Life* (Second Edition)
Ed Boenisch, Ph.D. and C. Michele Haney, Ph.D.
Softcover: $15.95   224 pages
New edition of the popular, practical guide to stress management with self-assessment charts covering people, money, work, leisure stress areas. Life-changing strategies to enhance relaxation and serenity.

Is That All There Is? Balancing Expectation and *Disappointment in Your Life*
David Brandt, Ph.D.
Softcover: $15.95   224 pages
Dr. Brandt explains the psychology of disappointment, social influences that contribute to it, ways we deal with it, and how to convert it to a force for positive growth in our lives.

How You Feel Is Up To You
The Power of Emotional Choice (Second Edition)
Gary D. McKay, Ph.D. and Don Dinkmeyer, Ph.D.
Softcover: $14.95   272 pages
New second edition shows you how to take responsibility for your emotions and choose how you feel. Step-by-step methods to turn feelings into assets.

Impact 🐌 Publishers®
POST OFFICE BOX 6016, ATASCADERO, CALIFORNIA 93423-6016
www.impactpublishers.com

Please see the following page for more books.

More Books With *Impact*

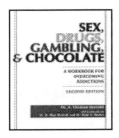